AVIATION LAW
FOR PILOTS

AVIATION LAW
FOR PILOTS

S. E. T. Taylor

and

H. A. Parmar

Eighth Edition

Revised by

R. B. Underdown

FRMetS, MRAeS
formerly Director of Ground Training and latterly Principal,
College of Air Training, Hamble

OXFORD

BLACKWELL SCIENTIFIC PUBLICATIONS

LONDON EDINBURGH BOSTON

MELBOURNE PARIS BERLIN VIENNA

Blackwell Scientific Publications
Editorial Offices:
Osney Mead, Oxford OX2 0EL
25 John Street, London WC1N 2BL
23 Ainslie Place, Edinburgh EH3 6AJ
238 Main Street, Cambridge,
  Massachusetts 02142, USA
54 University Street, Carlton
  Victoria 3053, Australia

First published in Great Britain by
  Crosby Lockwood & Son Ltd 1971
Reprinted 1973
Second edition 1974
Third edition 1978
Fourth edition published by Granada
  Technical Books 1983
Fifth edition published by Collins
  Professional and Technical Books 1986
Sixth edition published by
  BSP Professional Books 1988
Reprinted 1989
Seventh edition published by
  BSP Professional Books 1989
Seventh edition revised 1990
Eighth edition published by
  Blackwell Scientific Publications 1993

Set by DP Photosetting, Aylesbury, Bucks
Printed and bound in Great Britain by
Hartnolls Ltd, Bodmin, Cornwall

DISTRIBUTORS

Marston Book Services Ltd
PO Box 87
Oxford OX2 0DT
(*Orders:* Tel: 0865 791155
        Fax: 0865 791927
        Telex: 837515)

USA
Blackwell Scientific Publications, Inc.
  238 Main Street
  Cambridge, MA 02142
  (*Orders:* Tel: 800 759-6102
          617 225-0401)

Canada
Oxford University Press
70 Wynford Drive
Don Mills
Ontario M3C 1J9
(*Orders:* Tel: 416 441-2941)

Australia
Blackwell Scientific Publications Pty Ltd
54 University Street
Carlton, Victoria 3053
(*Orders:* Tel: 03 347-5552)

British Library
Cataloguing in Publication Data

A catalogue record for this book is
available from the British Library

ISBN 0-632-03502-1

Library of Congress
Cataloging in Publication Data

Taylor, S.E.T. (Sydney Ernest Thomas)
    Aviation law for pilots / S.E.T. Taylor
  and H.A. Parmar.—8th ed. / revised by
  R.B. Underdown.
      p.   cm.
    Includes index.
    ISBN 0-632-03502-1
    1. Aeronautics—Law and legislation—
  Great Britain.   I. Parmar, H.A.
  (Hasmukhlal Amritlal)   II. Underdown,
  R.B.   III. Title.
  KD2720.T38   1993
  343.4109'7'0246291—dc20
  [344.103970246291]   92-29970
                                            CIP

Contents

Preface to Eighth Edition

Aviation law with its associated flight rules and procedures has always been a daunting subject for the aspiring pilot and rightly so in view of its importance in the safe operation of aircraft. Legislation is always evolving and following the United Kingdom's signature of the Treaty of European Unity in February 1992, paving the way for a common European market from January 1993, new syllabuses for pilots' licences have been introduced.

The European Civil Aviation Conference through wide consultations within and between its member states has produced harmonised syllabuses setting the required standards. National governments, by ratifying the agreements, implement these standards throughout Europe. In the case of the United Kingdom the main legislation is embodied in the Air Navigation Order and its amendments with detailed procedures, tables, frequencies etc. being formally promulgated in the UK Air Pilot (UK AIP).

The earlier editions of *Aviation Law for Pilots* first tackled the task of interpreting the legal jargon. This new edition has been substantially rewritten to embody all recent developments but nevertheless every effort has been made to retain the familiar style.

Aviation law is an important subject for every aspiring pilot whether private or professional. It is a 'once-only' affair for the student seeking a professional pilot's licence. Once the law examination papers have been passed at the Basic Commercial Pilot's Licence level, the subject is not then re-examined when converting to a higher level.

This volume covers the entire syllabus. Although the law content of the Private Pilot's Licence (PPL) syllabus has been considerably expanded in recent years, its scope is narrower than that required for a professional licence. Unless specially noted at the chapter heading, the chapters and paragraphs marked with an asterisk (*) may be omitted by those studying for their PPL.

Roy Underdown
Hamble, Hants
August 1992

Abbreviations

AAL, aal	–	Above aerodrome level
ABN	–	Aerodrome Beacon
A/c, a/c	–	Aircraft
ACC	–	Area Control or Area Control Centre
ADA	–	Advisory Airspace
ADF	–	Automatic Direction Finder
ADR	–	Advisory Route
ADT	–	Approved Departure Time
AFIS	–	Aerodrome Flight Information Service
AFS	–	Aeronautical Fixed Service
AFTN	–	Aeronautical Fixed Telecommunication Network
agl	–	Above Ground Level
AIC	–	Aeronautical Information Circular
AIP	–	Aeronautical Information Publication
AIREP	–	Air Report
AIS	–	Aeronautical Information Service
amsl	–	Above Mean Sea Level
ANO	–	Air Navigation Order
ASR	–	Altimeter Setting Region
ATAS	–	Air Traffic Advisory Service
ATC	–	Air Traffic Control
ATCC	–	Air Traffic Control Centre
ATCU	–	Air Traffic Control Unit
ATFM	–	Air Traffic Flow Management
ATIS	–	Automatic Terminal Information Service
ATS	–	Air Traffic Service
ATSU	–	Air Traffic Service Unit
Authority	–	Civil Aviation Authority
AUW	–	All-up Weight
AWY	–	Airway
C	–	Degrees Celsius
CAA	–	Civil Aviation Authority
CANP	–	Civil Aircraft Notification Procedure
CAS	–	Controlled Airspace
CEU	–	Central Executive Unit (Flow management)
C of A	–	Certificate of Airworthiness
CTMO	–	Central Traffic Management Organisation

CTR	–	Control Zone
DA	–	Decision Altitude
DF	–	Direction Finding
DH	–	Decision Height
DME	–	Distance Measuring Equipment
DR	–	Dead Reckoning
EAT	–	Expected Approach Time
ECAC	–	European Civil Aviation Conference
ED	–	Emergency Distance
EET	–	Estimated Elapsed Time
ELT	–	Emergency Location Transmitters
EPIRB	–	Emergency Position Indicating Radio Beacons
ETA	–	Estimated Time of Arrival
F	–	Degrees Fahrenheit
FAL	–	Facilitation of International Air Transport
FAX	–	Facsimile Transmission
FIR	–	Flight Information Region
FIS	–	Flight Information Service
FL	–	Flight Level
FLG	–	Flashing
FMU	–	Flight Management Unit
GASIL	–	General Aviation Safety Information Leaflet
GCA	–	Ground Controlled Approach
H24	–	Continuous Day and Night Service
HDG, Hdg	–	Heading
HF	–	High Frequency (3000–30 000 KHz)
Hr, hr	–	Hour
Hz, Hz	–	Hertz (cycle per second)
IAS	–	Indicated Air Speed
IBN	–	Identification Beacon
ICAO	–	International Civil Aviation Organisation
ID	–	Identification
IFR	–	Instrument Flight Rules
ILS	–	Instrument Landing System
IMC	–	Instrument Meteorological Conditions
ISA	–	International Standard Atmosphere
JAA	–	Joint Aviation Authorities
JAR	–	JAA Requirements
KG, kg	–	Kilogram(s)
KHZ, KHz	–	Kilohertz
KM, Km	–	Kilometre(s)
KT, Kt	–	Knot(s)
LARS	–	Lower Airspace Radar Advisory Service
LATCC	–	London Air Traffic Control Centre
LDA	–	Landing Distance Available
LF	–	Low Frequency (30–300 KHz)
M	–	Mach Number (followed by figures)

M, m	–	Metre(s)
MATZ	–	Military Air Traffic Zone
mb	–	Millibars
MEHT	–	Minimum Eye Height over Threshold
METAR	–	Aviation routine weather report (in code)
MF	–	Medium Frequency (300–3000 KHz)
MHz	–	Megahertz
MIN, min	–	Minute(s)
MNP	–	Minimum Navigation Performance
M.o.D.	–	Ministry of Defence
MOTNE	–	Meteorological Operational Telecommunications Network Europe
Ms	–	Minus
MTWA	–	Maximum Take-off Weight Authorised
MWO	–	Meteorological Watch Office
NAPs	–	Noise Abatement Procedures
NATS	–	National Air Traffic Services
NDB	–	Non-directional Beacon
NM, nm	–	Nautical Mile(s)
NOSIG	–	No significant change
OCA	–	Shanwick Oceanic Control Area
OCC	–	Occluding (light)
OCL	–	Obstacle Clearance Limit
Order	–	Air Navigation Order
PANS	–	Procedures for Air Navigation Services
PAR	–	Precision Approach Radar
PAX	–	Passengers
R.B.	–	Relative Bearing
RCC	–	Rescue Co-ordination Centre
Regs.	–	Regulations
RFP	–	Repetitive Flight Plan
RIS	–	Radar Information Service
RLCE	–	Request Level Change en route
RNAV	–	Area Navigation
RNLI	–	Royal National Life Boat Institution
ROAR	–	Rules of the Air Regulations
RP	–	Reporting Point
RTF	–	Radiotelephony
RTG	–	Radiotelegraphy
RTOW	–	Regulated Take-off Weight
RVR	–	Runway Visual Range
RWY	–	Runway
SAR	–	Search and Rescue
SARP	–	ICAO Standards and Recommended Practices
SARSAT	–	Search and Rescue Satellite Aided Tracking System
Sch.	–	Schedule
SELCAL	–	Selective Calling System

SFC	–	Surface
SID	–	Standard Instrument Departure
SIGMET	–	Message of occurrence or expected occurrence of certain hazardous phenomena
SNOCLO	–	Closed by snow
SNOWTAM	–	Special message notifying of snow-affected movement areas
SPECI	–	Aviation Selected Special Weather Report (in code)
SPL	–	Supplementary flight plan message
SSR	–	Secondary Surveillance Radar
STAR	–	Standard Instrument Arrival
SVFR	–	Special Visual Flight Rules
TA	–	Transition altitude
TAF	–	Aerodrome Forecast
TAS	–	True Airspeed
T.B.	–	True Bearing
TMA	–	Terminal Control Area
TODA	–	Take-off Distance Available
TORA	–	Take-off Run Available
TRLVL	–	Transition level
TVOR	–	Terminal VOR
TWR	–	Aerodrome Control or Tower
UHF	–	Ultra High Frequency (300–3000 MHz)
UIR	–	Upper Flight Information Region
UK	–	United Kingdom
U/S	–	Unserviceable
UTC	–	Co-ordinated Universal Time
VASIS	–	Visual Approach Slope Indicators
VFR	–	Visual Flight Rules
VHF	–	Very High Frequency
VLF	–	Very Low Frequency (3–30 KHz)
VLR	–	Very Long Range
VMC	–	Visual Meteorological Conditions
VOR	–	Very High Frequency Omni Range
VSTOL	–	Very short take-off and landing
VTOL	–	Vertical take-off and landing
WEF/wef	–	With effect from
WIP	–	Work in progress
WPT	–	Waypoint

1
International Legislation

Whether an aircraft is being flown around a small grass field or on an international journey, flights will only be conducted safely if certain basic rules are observed. In this, aviation is no different from other forms of transport such as the road or the sea. As aviation activities have developed, so the procedures and practices to accommodate change have had to evolve too. There was even an international agreement on the conduct of aerial activities before the Wright brothers made their first flight and Bleriot flew the English Channel. As in almost all other spheres, aviation law both nationally and internationally has its own jargon, acronyms and organisations generally known by their initials. Probably the most commonly used throughout this volume are CAA – the Civil Aviation Authority of the United Kingdom – and ICAO – the International Civil Aviation Organisation.

The greatest impetus for conformity and regulation of aviation came as an outcome of the two world wars of 1914–1918 and 1939–1945. After World War 1 the League of Nations came into being as an international authority and the specialised agency The International Commission for Air Navigation (ICAN) was established to provide for the safe and efficient navigation of aircraft. Apart from bringing together the various national aviation authorities and their operating practices, ICAN also postulated a standard atmosphere by which aircraft performance could be measured and against which aircraft instruments could be calibrated. It also had an ambitious programme to map the whole of the globe for aviation purposes, including a common base scale and using a common chart projection.

The changes in World War 2, with the advent of the jet engine and advances in aircraft design and equipment, enormously increased ranges and reliability, and brought renewed international co-operation for civil aviation even before war had ended. In December 1944, at a convention in Chicago, USA, the pattern was set for the regulation of post-war civil aviation. Initially 52 nations attended and laid down the foundations for the standardisation of operating procedures and navigation practices of international air transport. Such international agreements then have to be ratified by the various individual national legislatures, so until sufficient countries had carried out this process, Chicago established a Provisional Civil Aviation Organisation (PICAO). In due course ICAO came into being and co-ordinates advancement particularly of the technicalities of international air navigation and of air safety.

The Convention on International Civil Aviation has a number of Annexes which range from Personnel Licensing to the Transport of Dangerous Goods by

Air. The content of those annexes relevant to the professional pilot's licence syllabus – noted below – is covered in the various chapters which follow but, for convenience of continuity, not in the numerical sequence of the annexes.

Annex 1   Personnel Licensing
Annex 2   Rules of the Air
Annex 7   Aircraft Nationality and Registration Marks
Annex 9   Facilitation
Annex 11   Air Traffic Services
Annex 12   Search and Rescue
Annex 13   Aircraft Accident Investigation
Annex 14   Aerodromes
Annex 15   Aeronautical Information Service
Annex 17   Security
Annex 18   Transport of Dangerous Goods by Air.

ICAO has its headquarters permanently based in Montreal, Canada. However, the terrain over which aircraft operate varies from desolate polar regions to equatorial jungle and from highly populated industrial areas to wide expanses of open ocean or desert. The consequential need for provision of navigational facilities and air traffic procedures also varies with locality around the globe. To handle this, ICAO has a number of regional offices and in addition to the worldwide standard Procedures for Air Navigation Services (PANS) there are regional supplementary procedures together with regional air navigation planning. In the case of Europe, national legislation is guided by the European Community (EC) together with consultations within the European Civil Aviation Conference (ECAC) and its subsidiary body Joint Aviation Authorities (JAA) which develop measures which ensure uniformly high standards of airworthiness through Joint Aviation Requirements (JARs) and Eurocontrol.

In framing its wording of the text of the Annexes to the Convention, ICAO deliberately resolved to draw contracting states' attention to the desirability of using in their own national regulations, as far as practicable, the precise language of those ICAO standards that are of a 'regulatory character' by emphasising that wherever possible the provisions of Annex have been written in such a way as to facilitate incorporation, without major textual changes, into national legislation. In fact, ICAO set out both 'Standards' and 'Recommended Practices' (SARPs).

A Standard is any specification for physical characteristics, configuration, materiel, performance, personnel or procedures, the uniform application of which is recognised as necessary for the safety or regularity of international air navigation and to which contracting states will conform in accordance with the Convention; in the event of impossibility of compliance, notification to the Council is compulsory under Article 18.

A Recommended Practice is any specification for physical characteristics, configuration, materiel, performance, personnel or procedures, the uniform application of which is recognised as desirable in the interest of safety, regularity or efficiency of international air navigation, and to which contracting states will endeavour to conform in accordance with the Convention.

Where the United Kingdom is unable to comply with a standard or recommended practice it notifies ICAO and lists its departure from the ICAO standard in the UK Aeronautical Information Publication (AIP), the Air Pilot, usually at the beginning of the appropriate section.

Through the International Air Transport Agreement, 'Freedoms of the Air' were established. The first two freedoms have become known as 'technical rights' to differentiate them from numbers 3, 4, and 5 called 'traffic rights'. For an aircraft registered in, say, State A, the five freedoms may be defined as:

First freedom   –   The privilege of flying over the territory of another State B without landing.

Second freedom   –   The privilege of landing in State B for technical reasons only.

Third freedom   –   The privilege to set down in State B, passengers, cargo and mail loaded in State A.

Fourth freedom   –   The privilege of picking up in State B, traffic destined for State A.

Fifth freedom   –   The privilege of picking up or setting down in State B traffic which is destined for or has been picked up in State C.

This fifth freedom has subsequently had slight variations evolve from its original form, sometimes known as sixth and seventh freedoms, but traffic rights have been the subject of much international and political debate. The Chicago Convention recognises that every state has complete and exclusive sovereignty over the airspace above its territory, hence the difficulty of nations agreeing 'open skies' policies.

Another important international development was the Tokyo Convention held in 1963. This convention came about because by that date the number of incidents such as 'hijacks' had increased so much that ICAO states decided to hold a 'Convention on Offences and Certain Other Acts committed on board Aircraft'. The Tokyo Convention determined that signatory states would adopt appropriate measures to achieve three main aims, should such offences or acts be perpetrated. The aims are:

(1) to restore control of the aircraft to the lawful undertaking;
(2) to permit the passengers to continue their journey;
(3) to return the aircraft to the lawful owner.

As already mentioned, Annex 17 deals with Security and this is covered in greater detail in Chapter 18.

Moving from international legislation to national legislation, as already mentioned, in the case of the United Kingdom civil aviation legislation is based on the principles, standards and recommended practices established before and after ICAO through successive Civil Aviation Acts and associated Acts of Parliament. Under these Acts, Orders, e.g. The Air Navigation Order, are laid before Parliament and are amended whenever they need updating. In turn, the

Air Navigation Order (ANO), formally through its 'Articles', establishes the authority for the United Kingdom Air Pilot and NOTAMs together with the official 'notification' of information, facilities, procedures etc. By powers under the ANO the Secretary of State for Transport is empowered to make Regulations, e.g. Rules of the Air Regulations (RoAR), which get down to the detailed rules with which pilots must comply. It is against the background of the internationally agreed general principles and practices that the detailed procedures and rules applicable in the United Kingdom have been developed. These are set out in the following chapters.

2
VFR/IFR

All airspace is basically divided into two categories – Controlled Airspace (CAS) and Uncontrolled Airspace – with different rules of flight applying to each. There are two fundamental flight rules called VFR and IFR. Flight is only permitted subject to one of these two rules. VFR stands for 'Visual Flight Rules' and a VFR Flight means a flight conducted in accordance with visual flight rules, while an IFR Flight means a flight conducted in accordance with the instrument flight rules.

A pilot may fly IFR at any time at his option (providing certain criteria are met) and there are certain situations in which one must fly IFR. All flying at night is under IFR. There are particular situations in which a pilot can fly VFR. The rules are governed by two factors: the type of airspace in which the flight is to take place and the weather conditions prevailing. There are in fact seven classes of airspace laid down by ICAO, lettered from A to G. Of these, A to E are Controlled Airspace.

The factors and the classes are shown in Table 2.2 for ready comparison. The term 'Flight Visibility' used in the tables is defined as 'Visibility forward from the flight deck of an aircraft in flight'. The weather conditions defined in the tables as enabling one to fly VFR are known as Visual Meteorological Conditions (VMC) and in the UK are as given in Table 2.1 below. (Privileges of licences/ratings may modify these.) On a VFR flight the pilot undertakes complete responsibility for the safe conduct of his flight. He is required to maintain flight separation from other aircraft flying in his area, navigate his aircraft and so forth. The Air Traffic Control (ATC) does not give him any clearances or instructions; there is no control exercised over him from the ground and he is generally left with a lot of freedom of action.

Minimum height for IFR

Irrespective of the class of Airspace, unless an aircraft is being flown on a notified route or is taking off or landing, or has been otherwise authorised by the appropriate ATS unit or is flying at an altitude not above 3000 ft amsl and clear of cloud and in sight of the surface, the pilot must ensure that the aircraft is flown to maintain ground clearance of at least 1000 ft above the highest obstacle within 5 nm.

Quadrantal/semi-circular height rules

In the UK, in order to comply with IFR, when flying outside controlled airspace

Table 2.1   VMC in the UK

Flight Level	Flight Visibility	Distance from cloud for airspace class	
At and above FL 100	8 km	(a) Class B	– clear of cloud
		(b) Classes D, E, F and G	– Horiz. 1500 m – Vert. 1000 ft
Below FL 100	5 km	(a) Classes D, E, F and G	– Horiz. 1500 m – Vert. 1000 ft
		(b) Classes F & G at or below 3000 ft amsl	– (i) Horiz. 1500 m Vert. 1000 ft or (ii) Clear of cloud and in sight of the surface*

* Flight visibility minima 1500 m at IAS 140 kt or less, but helicopters may operate in flight visibilities less than 1500 m at a speed which, having regard to visibility, is reasonable.

Notes:
(1) FL – Flight Level. (See Chapter 4.)
(2) Maximum Indicated Airspeed (IAS) is 250 knots for non-military flights below FL 100 except in airspaces Class A, B and C. (At present, the UK has no Class C airspace.)
(3) In these criteria, the UK departs slightly from the ICAO standard which requires aircraft below 3000 ft for VFR flight to be in sight of the surface.

in IMC, aircraft in level flight must be flown at the appropriate cruising level. (For meaning of the term 'flight level' see Chapter 4.) The levels allocated, based on a pressure setting of 1013.2 millibars, depend on the direction of the Magnetic Track of the aircraft, and are as follows:

Flight at levels below 24 500 ft
Magnetic Track between 000 and 089 (inc) – Fly at odd thousand feet, e.g., 5000, 7000 etc.

between 090 and 179 (inc) – Fly at odd thousand plus 500 feet, e.g., 5500, 7500 etc.

between 180 and 269 (inc) – Fly at even thousand feet, e.g., 4000, 6000 etc.

between 270 and 359 (inc) – Fly at even thousand feet plus 500 feet, e.g., 4500, 6500 etc.

This rule is known as the Quadrantal Rule since the flight level depends on the quadrant of the circle where the flight is taking place. Perhaps the rule is more easily remembered from the diagram shown in Fig. 2.1 (Note: 24 500 is not used.)

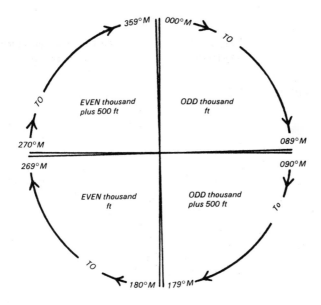

Fig. 2.1   Magnetic tracks.

Flight above 24 500 feet
The following semi-circular rule applies:

Magnetic Track between 000 and 179 (inc). Levels available are:
   25 000
   27 000
   29 000
   33 000 and every 4000 ft thereafter.

Magnetic Track between 180 and 359 (inc). Levels available are:
   26 000
   28 000
   31 000
   35 000 and every 4000 ft thereafter.

Quadrantals and semi-circular levels are flown with 1013.2 mb set on the altimeter subscale and their aim is to provide separation between conflicting traffic in IFR. They *must* be flown when outside controlled airspace in IFR and pilots are *advised* to fly quadrantals in VFR.

Under the quadrantal rules, 1000 ft separation is provided between two aircraft on reciprocal magnetic tracks. For example, if an aircraft on a track of 087(M) is flying at flight level 70 (that is, 7000 ft indicated, with a subscale setting of 1013.2 mb) another aircraft on the reciprocal track of 267(M) will be flying either at FL 60 or 80. Under semi-circular rules, 1000 ft separation is provided up to 29 000 ft and 2000 ft separation above that.

Table 2.2 UK airspace classifications

	Controlled airspace					Uncontrolled airspace	
	Class A	Class B	Class C	Class D	Class E	Class F	Class G
For IFR flights							
Separation	All aircraft	All aircraft	IFR from IFR IFR from VFR	IFR from IFR	IFR from IFR	IFR from IFR (participating IFR traffic)	Not provided (but see note)
Service(s)	Air Traffic Control Service (ATC)	ATC	ATC	ATC, including traffic information about VFR flights (and traffic avoidance advice on request)	ATC and traffic information about VFR flights as far as practical	Air traffic advisory service Flight information service (FIS)	FIS (see note)
Speed limitations	← Not applicable →			← Below FL 100 – IAS 250 kt →			
Radio	← Required →			← Not required →			
ATC clearance	← Required →			← Not required →			
For VFR flights							
Separation	←	All aircraft	VFR from IFR	Not provided	Not provided	Not provided (see note)	Not provided (see note)

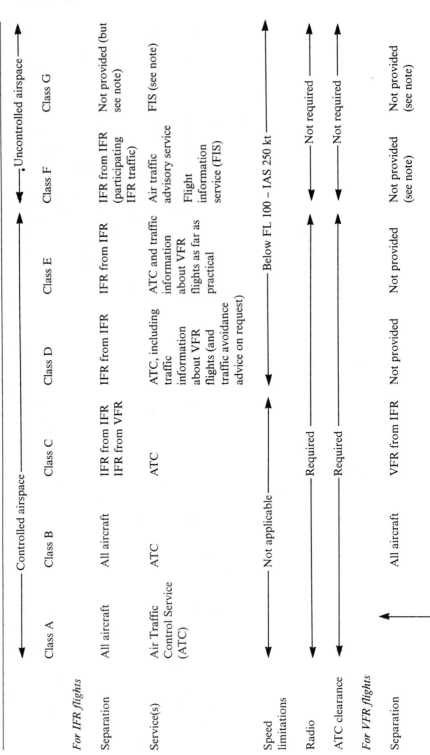

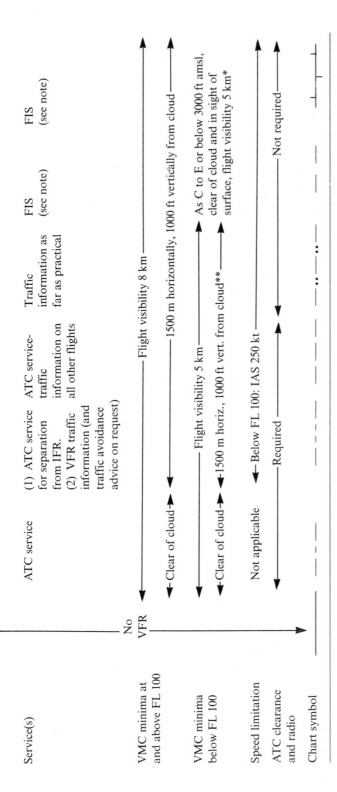

Service(s)		ATC service	(1) ATC service for separation from IFR. (2) VFR traffic information (and traffic avoidance advice on request)	ATC service-traffic information on all other flights	Traffic information as far as practical	FIS (see note)	FIS (see note)
	No	VFR					
VMC minima at and above FL 100			Flight visibility 8 km ————————				
		Clear of cloud	1500 m horizontally, 1000 ft vertically from cloud				
VMC minima below FL 100			Flight visibility 5 km		As C to E or below 3000 ft amsl, clear of cloud and in sight of surface, flight visibility 5 km*		
		Clear of cloud — 1500 m horiz., 1000 ft vert. from cloud**					
Speed limitation		Not applicable	Below FL 100: IAS 250 kt				
ATC clearance and radio		Required		Not required			
Chart symbol							

Note: The Separation and Services provisions shown in the table are the minimum to meet ICAO Standards and Recommended Practices (SARPs) and may be supplemented where practicable. Class F and Class G often have Radar Advisory Service (RAS) and Radar Information Service (RIS) available from Air Traffic Service units which pilots are urged to use. (See Chapter 10.)

* At 140 kt IAS or less, flight is permitted in flight visibilities down to 1500 m. Helicopters may operate in less than 1500 m flight visibility at a speed which is reasonable in regard to the visibility.

** Exemption permits aircraft to fly visual circuits in classes D and E Airspaces at cloud bases less than 1000 ft above circuit height, by permitting flight by such aircraft at or below 3000 ft amsl at a speed of 140 kt IAS or less which remain clear of cloud, in sight of the surface and in a flight visibility of at least 5 km. Helicopters may fly VFR in Class D or E Airspace at or below 3000 ft amsl clear of cloud and in sight of the surface.

Special VFR (SVFR)

From the rules of VFR and IFR discussed above, it will be apparent that a pilot who is unable to fulfil IFR requirements cannot:

(1) enter controlled airspace in IMC (full IFR procedures necessary) or at night (no VFR at night);
(2) enter controlled airspace either by day or night, irrespective of weather conditions, if that controlled airspace is notified for the purpose of rule 21;
(3) enter any airspace to which special rules apply.

When it is necessary to undertake a flight in the above areas and the pilot is unable to comply with IFR he may apply for a Special VFR clearance. In connection with Special VFR the following points should be noted. Before requesting a Special VFR a pilot must ensure that:

(1) he can fly at such a height as will enable him to land clear of a built-up area in the event of engine failure;
(2) the requisite flight visibility can be maintained;
(3) his responsibility regarding terrain clearance can be met.

Thus, ATC may impose height restrictions, may deny a special VFR, and a pilot may not accept the clearance offered. An alternative course of action should therefore be prepared. ATC will not issue a Special VFR clearance to any fixed wing aircraft intending to depart from an aerodrome within a Control Zone when the official meteorological visibility at that aerodrome is 1800 m or less or the cloud ceiling is less than 600 ft. Remember:

(1) A grant of such flight clearance is a concession and a pilot cannot claim it as of right.
(2) If and when the clearance is given, the flight takes place according to the special instructions issued by the ATC and not in accordance with IFR.
(3) Generally these flights take place in control zones or special rules areas (to be explained in the next chapter) at low altitudes. There is a rule of low flying when in the vicinity of a town, city or settlement that the aircraft must maintain a height of at least 1500 ft above the highest fixed object within 2000 ft of the aircraft (see Chapter 11). A pilot flying special VFR under ATC instructions is absolved from compliance with this rule, but not the rule mentioned above of being able to land clear of a congested area without danger to persons or property on the ground should an engine fail.
(4) There is no need to file a flight plan. All that is required are brief details comprising the aircraft's registration and callsign, aircraft type, pilot's intentions and a request for special VFR clearance. A flight plan may, however, be filed if the pilot wishes the destination aerodrome to be notified of his movement. The details required above may be passed over the RTF at less busy aerodromes.
(5) The ATC will provide standard separation between all special VFR flights and between VFR flight and other aircraft operating under IFR.

(6) Special VFR flights will not normally be given a specific level to fly; they must always, however, remain clear of cloud and in sight of the ground or water. They will generally be instructed not to fly above a certain level.

(7) The pilot must comply with ATC instructions and must remain at all times in flight conditions which will enable him to determine his flight path and keep clear of obstructions. A special VFR clearance does not absolve the pilot from the responsibility of avoiding Aerodrome Traffic Zones (ATZ) unless prior permission to penetrate the ATZ has been obtained beforehand from the relevant ATC unit.

(8) A private pilot, however, will only be cleared for special VFR if he holds an IMC rating, unless the visibility is at least 10 km.

The ICAO definition of Special VFR refers specifically to meteorological conditions. The UK definition departs from ICAO in that it allows Special VFR flight in notified Class A Control Zones (i.e. mandatory IFR irrespective of meteorological conditions) and in other control zones in IMC or at night.

At some aerodromes inside control zones, there are entry/exit lanes established for local aircraft to fly in IMC without complying with full IFR procedures, and in most cases without having to obtain clearance or carry radio. The procedures for flying in these lanes are contained in the RAC section of UK AIP. Your syllabus does not call for any information with regard to particular aerodromes. The lanes are only mentioned here just in case you are wondering how a student pilot flies his first solo at an aerodrome inside controlled airspace. Aircraft flying out of aerodromes adjacent to a Control Zone boundary and wishing to enter the zone may obtain Special VFR clearance either by telephone before take-off or by RTF when airborne. However, all such requests must specify the ETA for the selected entry point and must be made 5–10 minutes beforehand.

There is usually a current yellow (OPS/ATS) Aeronautical Information Circular entitled 'Conduct of VFR flights within the United Kingdom'. Although the Aeronautical Information Service is dealt with later in Chapter 5, it is worth noting here that this AIC which was published at the behest of the International Civil Aviation Organisation collates the information applicable to VFR flights and comes with its own index.

3
Types of Airspace

All airspace over the UK is variously divided. To understand the whole concept of these divisions, it is necessary to look into the types of problems that are present in various parts of the country, as well as the different situations and circumstances in which flight might take place.

First of all, a control centre is needed on the ground, not only to *control* aircraft in the air but also to maintain a general supervision of activities in the sky and provide advisory service to aircraft in need. Any concept of a single such control centre for the whole country can be ruled out immediately as impracticable. In fact, the country has been divided into two geographical divisions in order to provide this type of ATC service. These divisions are London FIR/UIR and Scottish FIR/UIR.

The term FIR stands for Flight Information Region and it extends vertically upward, up to *but not including* FL 245 (that is, 24 500 ft indicated on the altimeter with its sub-millibar scale set to 1013.2). UIR stands for Upper Flight Information Region and includes all airspace *at and above* FL 245. Let us put this in tabular form (Fig. 3.1); we will build it up as we go along.

AIRSPACE

Lower Airspace	Upper Airspace
Below FL 245:	FL 245 and above:
London and	London and
Scottish FIR	Scottish UIR

Fig. 3.1

Under this scheme, an aircraft at, say, FL 90 flies in one of the two FIRs, whereas another aircraft at, say, FL 330 flies in one of the two UIRs. This basic division of the airspace is universal, although the limiting altitudes/flight levels may differ from country to country.

Now, taking the UK as a whole, it is easy to visualise that in some parts the air traffic concentration will be very high, whereas in the other parts, relatively thin. Cities like London, Manchester and Glasgow attract a flow of national and international traffic, not to mention an ever increasing number of business executives hopping between cities for conferences etc. Further, flying clubs, for reasons only known to themselves, seem to cluster around big towns and they claim their proportion of the sky with the rest of them. All this leads to one conclusion: where the traffic density is high, the aircraft must fly under various restrictions imposed by the ATC. They must comply with the basic rules and obey ATC instructions. In return, the responsibility for smooth flow of the traffic and separation of aircraft from one another will be undertaken by the ATC. The airspace where such restrictions are imposed is called 'Controlled Airspace' (CAS) and 'notified' as Class A, B, C, D or E Airspace. Details of all such notifications are found in the RAC section of the UK AIP; you are not required to memorise detailed information, of course.

Then there are parts of the country, like Puddle-under-the-Marsh District where nobody wants to go, where the traffic is thin and the above restrictions are not considered necessary. Here, the flier has relatively more freedom of the sky and such airspace, believe it or not, is called 'Uncontrolled Airspace'.

So now we have geographical divisions of FIR/UIR for air traffic control purposes, and within these FIRs/UIRs the airspace is either controlled or uncontrolled. We add this to our tabular picture (Fig. 3.2).

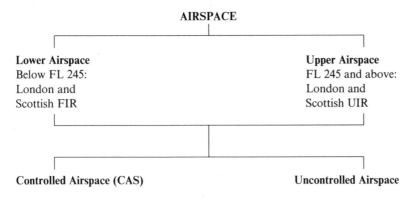

Fig. 3.2

Well, it might appear that this is the end of the story, but it is not. When we think of the control being exercised over aircraft movements we are immediately faced with the question of type of control, how far must the control extend, both horizontally and vertically and so on. These must essentially depend on the requirements peculiar to given circumstances. You guessed it right: there are going to be sub-divisions of the heading 'Controlled Airspace' (CAS).

Take a major aerodrome, say, Heathrow. Here, dense traffic is flowing in and out on a continuous basis, the movement taking place in a variety of directions. Therefore, in the interest of safety and the expeditious flow of air traffic, it is necessary for this aerodrome to have control over the traffic while aircraft are well away from the aerodrome boundary. Further, since aircraft land and take off here, the control is required to extend right from ground level. The control need not be exercised to unlimited altitude since we are only concerned with regulation of the traffic in the vicinity of the aerodrome. The airspace designated around such busy aerodromes for this purpose is called a *Control Zone* (*CTR*).

It may well have a complex shape.

A control zone may be defined as an 'airspace which has been notified as such within an FIR/UIR, within which air traffic control service is provided to IFR flights. It extends from the surface (SFC) to a specified altitude or flight level'.

From the definition it is clear that the *control service* is provided to IFR flights only. Thus, an aircraft flying under VFR may enter a CTR without any ATC control being exercised over it. Whether an aircraft may actually enter a zone under VFR will depend (as we pointed out above) on whether or not the zone is notified under rule 21 and/or 32.

O.K., let's get away from taking-off and landing at major aerodromes and consider the airspace linking major cities. Here, there is a regular traffic pattern and, where the traffic is dense enough, control service is again called for. You will note that we are not concerned here with control at ground level; our main interest is control at flight level. The airspace where such control is provided is called a *Control Area (CTA)*. The word 'area' stands in contrast with 'zone' since here we are interested in a flight from London to Manchester or Manchester to Glasgow, for example. A control area may be defined as an 'airspace which is notified as such within an FIR/UIR within which air traffic control service is provided to IFR flights. Control areas extend upward from a specified altitude or flight level and have no upper limit unless one is specified.' Control areas comprise:

(1) *Airways.* Airways do not extend to ground level and, therefore, they come within the definition of the control area. As for the control service to the aircraft, all national airways are notified for the purpose of rule 21. Therefore, no VFR traffic can take place on the airways. In the UK, airways are Class A Airspace (except where they pass through CTA, CTR or TMA of lesser status).

(2) *Terminal Control Areas (TMAs).* These are normally established at the confluence of airways in the vicinity of one or more major aerodromes. Their purpose is to sort out transit traffic from landing/departing traffic. Their importance lies in the fact that in their absence, all traffic would converge on the zone boundary irrespective of whether the aircraft wishes to land or transit through. With TMAs established, aircraft entering the TMA boundary and wishing to land, for example, may be routed on to the zone boundary; transit aircraft may be routed through a clearer area on to the other edge of the TMA boundary to continue on the next airway. Major TMAs are Class A Airspace. The AIP gives the class of airspace notified for TMAs in the UK.

So much for the controlled airspace. When we come to discuss the remainder of the airspace (i.e. uncontrolled airspace Classes F and G) we find that there are areas where there is sufficient traffic to call for separation service (that is, separation from conflicting traffic), but insufficient traffic to warrant full scale control. The areas where such partial service is available to aircraft voluntarily accepting the service are Class F Airspace, and if, within these areas, routes have been established, these routes are called *Advisory Routes (ADR)*.

Advisory Route

This is a designated route along which Air Traffic Advisory Service (ATAS) is available. Although depicted on UK aeronautical charts as a centre line, it takes the form of a corridor 10 nm wide (similar to an airway) extending from a specified level, with or without an upper limit.

An ADR is not controlled airspace and no control service is provided to flights operating in these areas. It is, however, a requirement that if the advisory service is required, the flight must be made under IFR flight plan. The term 'advisory service' in the above definition means normal Flight Information service plus separation service. The 'open' FIR is designated as Class G Airspace. More about these in Chapter 9.

Aerodromes have Aerodrome Traffic Zones (ATZ) established around them which are not allocated a specific class of airspace. They adopt the class of airspace within which they are located. (See also Chapter 9.) In Class G Airspace, Rule 39 of the Rules of the Air Regulations applies, but in Class A Airspace, for example, the more vigorous requirements of Class A take precedence but always incorporating the requirements of Rule 39. There are special rules for the Upper Heyford Mandatory Radio Area (Rule 40) which is in Class G Airspace. The rules are made to meet the local requirements and are checked through in the AIP before a flight is undertaken.

This leaves us with the rest of the country where the air traffic is less dense, and there is no call for either control service or the advisory service. Such airspace is again uncontrolled and the only ATC service normally available is what is called the Flight Information Service. Locally, an Air Traffic Control Service is normally established at aerodromes and operates within the aerodrome

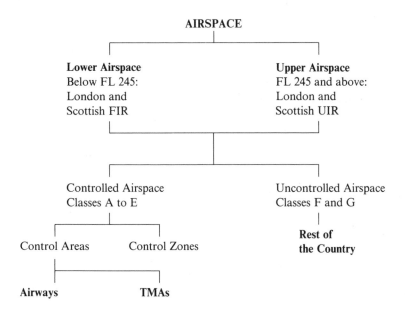

Fig. 3.3

boundary. We will be talking about conditions of flight in all these areas in Chapters 8 and 9. But we can now complete the picture in tabular form (Fig. 3.3).

(As a footnote it may be mentioned that in many countries all airspace is completely controlled. Although Jersey, Guernsey and the Isle of Man authorities have their own legislation, their rules for flight are compatible with those of the UK.)

Types of air traffic service units
Let us now examine how the air traffic control system copes with all this. The whole system is organised along the following lines.

(1) Air Traffic Control Centre (ATCC)
An ATCC combines the functions of an Area Control Centre (ACC) and Flight Information Centre. This means that within its area of jurisdiction it provides appropriate service to aircraft flying in both controlled and uncontrolled airspace. An Area Control Centre (ACC) is a term more common abroad and its function is to provide air traffic control to IFR flights. A Flight Information Centre is a unit established to provide flight information service and alerting service. An ATCC, combining the two above, provides the following services:

(a) Flight information service and alerting service.
(b) Advisory service to aircraft flying under IFR on the Advisory Service Routes.
(c) Area control service to aircraft on Airways and in TMAs.
(d) Area control service in some of the larger zones (e.g. London).

The pictorial representation in Fig. 3.4 will, hopefully, clarify the extent of the ATCC service.

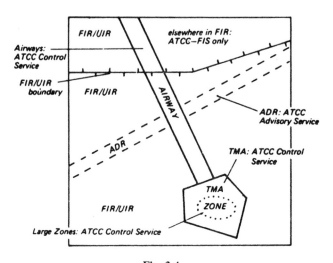

Fig. 3.4

(2) Zone Control Unit

These units are established at some of the zones, generally the zones of intermediate importance. They control the aircraft flying inside their zones. A zone controller does not control the take-off and landing phase of a flight.

(3) Aerodrome Control

(a) *Approach Control Unit.* This provides approach control service to aircraft taking off and landing under IFR. In small zones this unit also undertakes the function of the Zone Control Unit (e.g. Belfast Control Zone).

(b) *Aerodrome Control Unit.* This unit provides aerodrome control service at the aerodrome. It controls all local traffic whether in the air or on the ground.

To complete the picture, an aircraft taking off from an aerodrome inside a zone will undergo changes of control thus: aerodrome control, approach control, zone control, ATCC during flight in TMA (where in existence) and finally ATCC when flying along the airway.

Summary

Let us now regroup the salient points arising from the study of the first two chapters:

(1) If you are VMC, you may fly VFR, both in controlled airspace (unless it is notified for rules 21 and 32) and uncontrolled airspace. There is no VFR at night.

(2) In IMC you must fly IFR in controlled airspace. Outside controlled airspace you must fly at quadrantals if above 3000 ft. Note all the other requirements of IFR.

(3) Within FIRs/UIRs we have two main divisions: controlled airspace and uncontrolled airspace. Airways and TMAs are controlled areas. These, together with control zones, constitute controlled airspace.

(4) In uncontrolled airspace we have advisory routes where separation service is provided to aircraft flying on IFR flight plan. In the Upper Heyford Mandatory Radio Area special rules apply locally.

(5) The ATCCs provide communication service on an area basis to aircraft flying in controlled and uncontrolled airspace. ATCCs also provide control service in large zones.

4
Altimeter Setting Procedures

An altimeter reads the height of the aircraft by measuring the atmospheric pressure acting on its capsule and relating this to the datum set on the altimeter subscale. Thus, when flying at the same level, different height indications are obtained for different settings. There are three standard settings available from ATC for use in flight, each having a specific purpose of its own. These settings are named in the Q code and are explained below. The UK has elected to continue using the millibar, at least for the time being, as the unit of pressure. However, the alternative 'hectopascal' (which is identical in size, i.e. 1 millibar = 1 hectopascal) is an ICAO standard elsewhere.

QFE
This is the barometric pressure at the level of the aerodrome. When set, the altimeter reads the *height* above the aerodrome level.

An aerodrome surface may not be level, and the question arises as to what point on the aerodrome should be selected as the QFE reference point. The matter was standardised with the rule that the *aerodrome elevation* will be used as the QFE datum. Aerodrome elevation is defined as the highest point on the landing area. Therefore, QFE datum is the highest point on the landing area.

When QFE is set, the altimeter reads its height above the QFE datum. Thus, the setting is ideal for landing purposes if a near zero reading is desired on touchdown. When making a radar approach the ground controller presumes that you have QFE set. (At Army, RAF and USAF aerodromes different rules are applied). Since the QFE datum is the highest point on the landing area, where a precision runway is 7 ft or more below the QFE datum, the aerodrome barometric pressure to be passed to the landing aircraft will be the QFE *threshold elevation*.

QNH
This is the observed barometric pressure reduced to mean sea level in accordance with ISA (International Standard Atmosphere).

Since present day altimeters are also calibrated in ISA, when QNH is set on the subscale the correct 'height' above mean sea level is indicated. The technical name for this 'height' is '*altitude*'. Thus, if you are flying at, say, 2500 ft indicated with QNH set, then 2500 ft is your altitude. This setting is used as an alternative to QFE for take-off and landing purposes. The value passed by the controller for this purpose is generally known as 'aerodrome QNH'. This is only valid in the immediate vicinity of the issuing aerodrome.

Since, however, this setting indicates the aircraft's vertical displacement above mean sea level, it is very useful in determining terrain clearance when en route. For this purpose ATC or ATCC gives what is known as 'Regional QNH'. The UK airspace is divided into regions, called *Altimeter Setting Regions (ASRs)* and each region forecasts the lowest pressure value likely to prevail in that area per hour. A chart showing the distribution of ASRs is given in the UK AIP. New values are issued on change of the hour for the period H + 1 to H + 2 so a pilot can obtain regional QNH up to one hour ahead of the current hour, if required. This facility is particularly helpful to pilots undertaking a long cross country flight without radio. All QNH values obtained by radio must be read back.

In flight, a pilot needs to reset his altimeter to the new regional QNH after the initial setting on two occasions:

(1) on change of the hour if new values are forecast;
(2) when entering a new ASR.

Standard Setting

This is 1013.2 mb setting, and the aircraft flies *flight levels*. A flight level is simply the indication on the altimeter (with 1013.2 mb set) minus the last two zeros. Thus, an indication of 9000 ft is FL 90 and 27 500 ft is FL 275. The setting is used to provide separation from other traffic in the same airspace. All quadrantals and semi-circular heights are flown with this setting.

Definitions

We should now introduce a few definitions to lead us on to the study of the setting procedures.

Height is defined as the vertical distance of a level, point or object considered as a point, measured from a specified datum. It is also the vertical dimension of an object.

Altitude is the vertical distance of a level, point or object considered as a point from mean sea level.

Transition Altitude is the altitude in the vicinity of an aerodrome at or below which the vertical position of the aircraft is controlled by reference to altitude.

In the UK the transition altitude for aerodromes outside controlled airspace is generally 3000 ft. Within control zones, wherever possible, a common transition altitude is established for all aerodromes. The requisite information is 'notified' in the RAC section of the UK AIP and is also given on Instrument Approach Charts.

Transition Level is the lowest flight level available for use above the transition altitude.

Transition Layer is the airspace between transition altitude and transition level. On passing through the transition layer, climbing aircraft report their vertical position in terms of flight levels. Descending aircraft after vacating their flight level use the standard altimeter setting until no further FL reports are required.

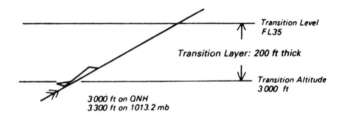

Transition Level
FL35

Transition Layer: 200 ft thick

Transition Altitude
3000 ft

3000 ft on QNH
3300 ft on 1013.2 mb

Fig. 4.1

The last three rather confusing definitions may perhaps be better understood with reference to Fig. 4.1.

An aircraft takes off with altimeter set to the aerodrome QNH which is, say, 1003 mb, and climbs with this setting until transition altitude is reached – 3000 ft. At this point, the climbing aircraft changes over to 1013.2 mb setting. Let's stop the aircraft at this point while the pilot alters the setting. Its new indication will now be:

Difference in setting = 1013 – 1003 = 10 mb.

Taking 1 mb = 30 ft, 10 mb = 300 ft and the new indication
= 3000 + 300 = 3300 ft

although the aircraft has not changed its level.

In order to reach the first quadrantal of 3500 ft, the aircraft must climb up another 200 ft. Therefore, 3500 ft or FL 35 is the transition level (lowest flight level available after transition altitude) and 200 ft is the vertical thickness of the transition layer.

Procedures
At the flight planning stage (discussed later) include the following:

(1) state the level either as FL number or altitude, as appropriate;
(2) level selected should ensure adequate terrain clearance, meet ATS require-ments and, where applicable, comply with quadrantal/semi-circular rule.

Rules within Controlled Airspace
(1) *Take-off.* At least one altimeter must be set to the aerodrome QNH.
(2) *Climb.* Reference to vertical position is passed in terms of altitude up to transition altitude, then as flight levels. However, after clearance to climb above transition level has been given, and provided that the aircraft is not more than 2000 ft below the transition altitude, vertical position is usually passed in terms of FL unless specifically instructed otherwise.
(3) *En route.* Fly flight levels at and above transition altitude. Use regional QNH for terrain clearance purposes. Aircraft flying in CTR/TMA at or below transition altitude are given the appropriate aerodrome QNH; regional QNH must not be used.
(4) *Approach and Landing*
    (a) Set aerodrome QNH when cleared to descend, unless further flight level

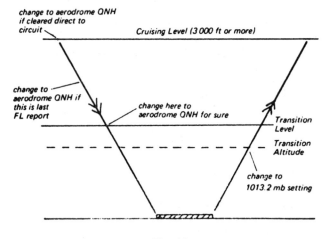

Fig. 4.2

vacating reports have been requested. In this case continue descending on 1013.2 mb until that flight level, make your report and see if you are finally cleared to circuit height. In any case, you must change over to aerodrome QNH at lowest flight level, at the latest. (See Fig. 4.2.)

(b) At final approach phase, set QFE or QNH at your option, but if you are making a radar approach the controller will presume that you have QFE set, and he will read out heights instead of altitudes (except at Army, RAF, USAF aerodromes initially). If you have QNH set for landing you must, therefore, specify this to the controller.

(c) Remember that the OCH (obstacle clearance height) is always given with reference to runway touchdown or aerodrome elevation.

(5) *Missed Approach.* If you have to carry out the missed approach procedure, you may continue on the setting you had on final approach but if during this phase you are required to report your vertical position, it must be given in terms of altitude only. This rule would recommend QNH setting on missed approach.

Rules outside Controlled Airspace

(1) *Take-off and initial climb.* Any desired setting.

(2) *Flight at and below 3000 ft:*

(a) You may fly with any desired setting but if the report of your vertical position is required, it must go out in terms of altitude.

(b) If you are flying along an ADR (Advisory Route) you must fly with regional QNH set.

(3) *Flight above 3000 ft.* Change over to 1013.2 mb on passing through the transition altitude when flying under IFR and conform to the quadrantal rule. Then report your position as flight level. If you are flying beneath a TMA or CTA, you should use the QNH of an aerodrome situated beneath that area.

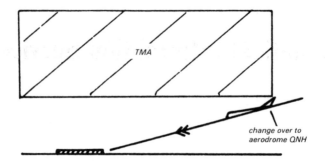

Fig. 4.3

(4) *Approach and Landing.* The rule is identical to approach and landing in controlled airspace.
(5) *Missed Approach.* The rule is the same as in controlled airspace.
(6) *Flight in TMAs.* When arriving or departing from aerodromes in TMA when at or below transition altitude, set aerodrome QNH (as against regional QNH). (See Fig. 4.3.)
(7) *Flight below TMAs.* When below transition altitude use the QNH of an aerodrome beneath the TMA and express vertical position as altitude.

Altimeter setting values
Altimeter settings are passed by the ATC to the pilot over the radio, rounded down to the nearest whole millibar. However, if a specific request is made, aerodrome pressure setting to the nearest tenth of a millibar will be given.

Pre-flight altimeter checks
In the UK, to enable the pilot to check the accuracy of his altimeter while on the apron, apron elevations are determined and displayed in the flight clearance office. They are also published in the UK AIP. The apron is also the designated place for altimeter checks.

5
Aeronautical Information Service

UK Air Pilot

All ICAO countries in accordance with Annex 15 publish aeronautical information of a practical operational nature in a document called 'Aeronautical Information Publication'. In the UK the AIP is given a specific name, the UK Air Pilot. The information contained in any AIP is arranged on a standard pattern so that once you know where a certain type of information is given in one country's AIP, you know where to look for the same type of information in any other AIP. There are also commercially produced 'Flight Guides' for national and international use in a format convenient for use on the flight deck.

The UKAIP is produced in the standard eight sections and it is an official document for 'notifying' the requirements of other aviation legislation. For example, rule 21 of the Rules of the Air Regulations says, 'In relation to flights in Visual Meteorological Conditions in Class A airspace, the commander of an aircraft shall comply with Rules 31 and 32 of these Rules as if the flight were IFR flight . . .'. This notification is made in the RAC section. The word 'notified' has been defined: it means, 'set forth in a document issued by the Authority and entitled "NOTAM-UK" or UK Air Pilot and for the time being in force'. Know this definition. The eight sections of the UKAIP are as follows:

AGA section. This contains information on aerodromes: classification and limitations on their use, hours of operation, availability of ground services, availability of Customs facilities, aerodrome lighting, Paved Runway Markings, Ground Signals, Use of Military Aerodromes and Snow Clearance Plans. On a map, all aerodromes listed in the section are shown.

Customs and sanitary airports for the use of international and commercial air transport are listed in full detail. This is followed by the Aerodrome Directory. Under this heading, tabulated information is given of all non-Customs aerodromes. This is followed by Special instructions, Restrictions, Warnings at individual aerodromes, e.g., Abingdon: Warning, caution necessary on approach to R/W 36; houses and television aerials form an obstruction, height 30 ft agl, 457 metres from touchdown.

Under another heading 'Obstruction and Safety Altitudes' you will find safety altitudes giving safe vertical clearance of 1000 ft above the highest known obstacle within 25 nm of the relevant aerodrome.

COM section. This section deals with communications and contains full information on radio communication and navigational services provided in this country. The table under the heading 'Radio Communication and Navigation Facilities' contains full details of various radio facilities available at each aerodrome. Succeeding pages contain information on other en route and long range navigational/communication facilities, including the broadcast of radio time signals, and airway frequencies.

MET section. This section contains information on the organisation of the meteorological service, procedures for aircraft operating on Air Routes, broadcasts of information for aircraft, and various meteorological codes. A list of meteorological offices available for use by civil pilots is included in Appendices.

RAC section. Rules of flight in various types of airspace, altimeter setting requirements, filing of flight plans, carriage of radio, airmiss reporting procedures, danger areas and other similar topics intimately connected with operational flying both inside and outside of controlled airspace are given in this section. It also lists the differences between UK and international procedures and definitions. It is a very large section indeed and there is a very useful index at the end of the RAC section, running to over 20 pages.

FAL section. Arrival, departure and transit procedures, aircraft documentation, customs, health, passenger documents, export and import of cargo and other similar aspects of flying are covered in this section.

SAR section. This section deals with search and rescue organisation and procedures.

MAP section. Gives details of various maps and charts available. Some countries use this section to publish their instrument procedure charts applicable to various aerodromes.

GEN section. This is a general section and contains a list of Civil Aviation Legislation, details of dimensional units, aircraft nationality and registration marks and a note on the time system. Some countries use this section to publish a list of abbreviations.

Keeping the UKAIP up to date

Because the UK conforms with Annex 15 it publishes an 'integrated package'. This means that the UKAIP is supported by the following amendments and supplements:

(1) *AIRAC (Regulated System for Air Information) Amendments.* These are published 4-weekly and give 6 weeks advance notice of changes that will occur on one particular date. Pilots thus know that only in exceptional cases will operationally significant changes occur on other dates. These amendments are mostly in the form of replacement pages for the AIP.
(2) *AIP Amendments (Non-AIRAC).* These are usually published as amendment pages every month and deal with non-operationally significant changes.

(3) *AIP Supplements (formerly NOTAMs II)*. These cover items of a temporary nature. To be included, changes must be of long duration (3 months) or supplementary information of operational significance, e.g. Air Exercises, major work in progress, Royal occasions, etc. These are issued fortnightly on green paper and should be kept in the AIP binders.

NOTAMs (Notices to Airmen)

All other information not covered by AIP supplements or amendments will be issued as a NOTAM on the Aeronautical Fixed Telecommunication Network (AFTN). NOTAMs will include operationally significant changes that need to be introduced at short notice. Such changes will be supplemented as appropriate by Amendments or Supplements.

Trigger NOTAMs

All operationally significant changes dealt with by amendments or supplements will additionally be 'flagged up' by NOTAMs giving an abbreviated description, effective date and the AIP reference. This ensures that the information will appear in the Pre-flight Information Bulletins.

System NOTAMs

As recommended by ICAO, the UK now uses the 'System' NOTAM format. Full details can be found in AERAD Supplements or Jeppesen Airways Manuals. System NOTAMs are so designed that the information can be extracted automatically by computers to produce the Pre-flight Information Bulletins.

Aeronautical information circulars (AICs)

These are issued monthly and contain administrative, operative, safety, amendments to UK airspace restrictions charts, and a catalogue of maps and charts, all on different coloured paper. They are all to draw the airman's attention to something now or impending without urgency. The pink circulars are on safety matters and usually take about three readings as they are stern lectures written by a Committee at the CAA, but certainly momentous. Have them sent free to your aerodrome address – if you have them sent home, cough up £10 to cover postage and packing, and probably more by the time you read this. Some AIC information is subsequently published in the UK AIP while the CAA consider other information sufficiently promulgated. AICs are lapsed on the fifth anniversary of their date of issue.

The Aeronautical Information Service (AIS)

AIS is a part of the National Air Traffic Service (NATS), its function being to collect, collate, edit and disseminate aeronautical information for the safety and efficiency of air navigation, and to receive post-flight information. It is organised on the following basis:

(1) *Headquarters.* This is located at Heathrow. It maintains records of all facilities. It initiates AIP supplements.
(2) *AIS Centres.* There are three divisions:
    Southern – Heathrow
    Northern – Manchester
    Scottish – Prestwick.
    The centres initiate NOTAMs relative to their respective areas.
(3) *Aerodrome Units.* These maintain varying degrees of aeronautical information, e.g. aeronautical information publications and NOTAMs.

6
Aerodromes – General

Limitations on the use of aerodromes

There are certain limitations on the use of aerodromes. These are as follows:

General limitation. Civil aircraft are not permitted to land at any aerodrome which is not listed in the UK AIP, except in case of genuine emergency. However, aircraft may land at these unlisted aerodromes with the special permission of the appropriate authority. The permission to land at these and at disused airfields is granted only in exceptional circumstances, e.g. convey a sick person or carry out a task of national importance.

Government aerodromes. Permission is required before take-off to use a government aerodrome during published working hours. However, it is Ministry of Defence policy to encourage the use of active Government aerodromes by UK aircraft on inland flights. Outside published hours the aerodrome may be used by prior permission only in special circumstances.

Aerodrome licence, ordinary. The use of an aerodrome operating under this licence is with prior permission of the owner or the aerodrome manager.

Unlicensed aerodromes. Use of these aerodromes is with the prior permission of the owner.

Military aerodromes. If you wish to use a Service aerodrome, check that the aerodrome is open to civil traffic. Civil aircraft use is restricted to the normal hours of watch and to inland flights only. If it is available, check further if any limitations on traffic are imposed. Some aerodromes permit only a particular type or class of aircraft, e.g. private aircraft, chartered flight. All information is available in the AGA section of the UK AIP. In all cases their use is only with the prior permission of the Station Commander, and this permission must be obtained *before take-off.* In this respect they differ from other aerodromes where prior permission is necessary. Foreign aircraft may land at a Military aerodrome only if they are so diverted. With regard to the use of Military aerodromes, the following points should be noted:

(1) Report to the ATC on arrival and before leaving.
(2) Hangarage is provided only after Service requirements are met.
(3) The Service undertakes no responsibility for the provision of messing, accommodation, and the pilot may make his own arrangements regarding supply of fuel and oil, etc, after furnishing adequate cover against loss or

damage to Service property through the use of such equipment.

(4) The Service undertakes no liability for loss, damage or accident to the visitor's person or property.

(5) Use of Service apparatus, tractors, cranes, starter trolleys, chocks etc, is at the user's risk.

(6) Pilots making instrument approaches will be given 'Procedure Minimum' based on QNH (equivalent to OCA – Obstacle Clearance Altitude) and asked to state their Decision Altitude (DA) or Minimum Descent Altitude (MDA).

(7) Control of entry procedures apply to civil aircraft.

(8) Two-way RTF communication must be maintained. Generally the frequency is 122.10 MHz. VHF Emergency frequency of 121.5 must not be regarded as the common frequency and should only be used for an actual emergency. Light aircraft with no RTF may be treated exceptionally at the discretion of the Commanding Officer.

*Snow clearance plans

Many aerodromes in the UK take part annually in snow clearance plans in conjunction with Europe. A seasonal snow plan is usually published annually as an AIC before the onset of winter and it includes the following information:

(1) aerodromes where standard clearance will be carried out;
(2) equipment held at each aerodrome and the type of clearance;
(3) height and distance of snow banks permitted at each aerodrome;
(4) method of assessing braking action;
(5) authority to contact for current information;
(6) any local deviation from standard practice.

(1) Aerodrome responsibility

The participating aerodrome authority is responsible:

(1) for the clearance of snow on the aerodrome, the operational runway having first priority; prior alerting of the services;
(2) for measuring and reporting the aerodrome state.

(2) Clearance technique

Whenever possible, the runways should be cleared completely. Snow blowers/ sweeper should be used as soon as snow falls. Residual snow is cleared by snow plough and rotary brushes, followed by the snow blower. Slush and standing water is to be cleared when building up to 3 mm or more deep. Build up of snow banks is not allowed if it can be avoided. Non-toxic chemicals only may be used. Grit of crushed granite may be used to improve braking action. Priorities for clearance are as follows:

(a) main runway;
(b) run-up areas;

(c) aprons;
(d) taxiways;
(e) airport roads.

(3) Measurement and reporting
Measurements are taken of runway braking action, snow/slush depth, snow density and snow bank heights, as follows:

Runway braking action is assessed by the use of a continuous recording runway friction measuring trailer (Mu-meter) and the brake testing decelerometer (Tapley meter). Assessment of ice, snow and slush is reported as GOOD, MED-GOOD, MEDIUM, MED-POOR, POOR when the information is passed to the pilot. Wet runway condition is reported as GOOD, MEDIUM, POOR. The Tapley meter is used on ice and dry snow. The Mu-meter indicates the possibility of slush-planing when it gives a low value of coefficient of friction. Braking action will not be assessed in slush-planing conditions.

Depth measurement of snow/slush is carried out using a standard depth gauge. Depth information will be given in millimetres for each third of total runway length. Ice depth is not measured.

Snow density, assessed subjectively, is reported as DRY SNOW, WET SNOW, COMPACTED SNOW, SLUSH, STANDING WATER, ranging over a Specific Gravity (SG) from less than 0.35 to 1.00. On the ground, the terms are defined as:
  Dry snow is snow which can be blown if loose or, if compacted by hand, will fall apart again upon release. Specific gravity is up to but not including 0.35.
  Wet snow is snow which, if compacted by hand, will stick together and tend to or form a snowball. Specific gravity is 0.35 up to but not including 0.5.
  Compacted snow is snow which has been compressed into a solid mass that resists further compression and will hold together or break up into lumps if picked up. Specific gravity is 0.5 or over.
  Slush is water-saturated snow which with a heel-and-toe slap-down motion against the ground will be dispersed with a splatter. Specific gravity is 0.5 up to 0.8.

Snow banks are only reported when they exceed the height agreed initially.

(4) Frequency of reporting
Apart from information passed to the pilot over the RTF, regular reports are made by means of a special message called SNOWTAM at least once every 24 hours, or when a significant change takes place. Those connected to the MOTNE (Meteorological Operational Telecommunication Network, Europe) broadcast system will assess runway conditions every half hour.

(5) Availability of information
Information on the current state of snow clearance and on the condition of movement areas will be available from:

(a) designated authority at the aerodrome concerned;
(b) Aeronautical Information Service (AIS) at aerodromes;
(c) SNOWTAMS;
(d) locations served by the MOTNE system.

Pilots and operators are asked to make the maximum use of the information services created for the purpose and not to contact ATC for snow state information unless this is unavoidable.

Operations from contaminated runways

The general advice is that operations from runways contaminated with snow, slush or water should be avoided whenever possible. If an aerodrome despite all efforts cannot keep its operational runway cleared, a pilot if airborne should consider diversion to another aerodrome or, if still on the ground, delaying his take-off until conditions improve.

Apart from the runway surface condition as reported under the UK Snow Plan, water on the operational runway is reported to pilots as DAMP, WET (surface soaked but no visible patches of standing water), WATER PATCHES (visible and significant), FLOODED (visible extensive water patches).

It is the CAA's advice, in a pink Information Circular as referred to in Chapter 5, that depths greater than 3 mm of water, slush or wet snow, or 10 mm of dry snow, are likely to have a significant effect on the performance of aeroplanes, the main effects being:

(1) additional drag – retardation effects on the wheels and spray impingement drag;
(2) possibility of power loss or system malfunction due to spray ingestion or impingement;
(3) reduced wheel-braking performance – the problems of aquaplaning;
(4) directional control problems;
(5) possibility of structural damage.

Although the Airworthiness Division (AWD) of CAA is prepared to advise in cases of aircraft in particular performance groups, the recommended procedures for take-offs from contaminated runways include:

(1) Do not try to take off if the depth of:
    (a) water, slush or wet snow is greater than 15 mm;
    (b) dry snow is greater than 60 mm;
    (c) very dry snow is greater than 80 mm.
(2) Avoid the use of reverse thrust when manoeuvring on contaminated taxiways prior to take-off to avoid contamination of wing leading edges and adopt taxiing techniques which will avoid such/snow adherence to the airframe or accumulation around the flap/slot or landing gear areas.
(3) Consider all aspects when selecting the flap/slat configuration from the

range permitted in the Flight Manual and ensure all appropriate field length performance corrections are made.

(4) Do not carry unnecessary fuel.

(5) All devices on the aeroplane contributing to braking performance (tyres, reverse thrust, lift dump, etc.) should be serviceable. Check that the tyres are in good condition.

(6) Use maximum take-off power.

(7) Do not attempt to take off in tailwinds.

(8) Do not attempt to take off in a crosswind exceeding 10 knots.

(9) Use normal rotation and take-off safety speeds.

(10) Ensure that de-icing of the airframe and engine intakes, if appropriate, has been carried out, that the aircraft is aerodynamically clean at the time of take-off and pay meticulous attention to engine and airframe anti-ice drills.

(11) Use the maximum runway distance available. Keep to a minimum the amount of runway used to line up. Any significant loss should be deducted from the declared distances for the calculation of regulated take-off weight (RTOW).

AWD will advise on the safety of any proposed variation of these procedures.

Definitions in relation to aerodromes

Aerodrome elevation. The elevation is shown in the Aerodromes and Airport Schedules to the AGA section of the UK AIP, and is the elevation of the highest point on the landing area.

Alternate aerodrome. This is an aerodrome, selected prior to take-off, to which the flight may proceed when a landing at the intended destination becomes inadvisable.

*Supplementary aerodrome. This is an aerodrome to be used in special circumstances, e.g. when unable to use planned or alternate aerodrome.

*Declared distances. These include Take-off Run Available, Emergency Distance, Take-off Distance Available and Landing Distance. Each is defined as follows and may be better understood when read in conjunction with Fig. 6.1.

Take-off run available (TORA) is defined as the length of the declared take-off run which is available and suitable for the ground run of an aeroplane taking off.

Emergency Distance (ED) is defined as the length of the declared take-off run plus the length of the stopway available.

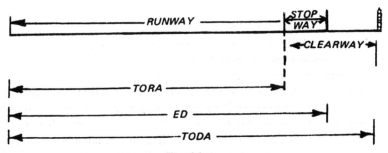

Fig. 6.1

Take-off Distance available TODA) is defined as the length of the declared take-off run plus the length of clearway available, or one and a half times TORA, whichever is the less.

Landing distance is defined as the length of runway (or surface when it is unpaved) which is available and suitable for the ground landing run of the aeroplane commencing at visual threshold markings or threshold lights. (In practice, where, in case of an unpaved landing area, no threshold markings are provided, the landing distance is measured from the junction of the surface with a 1:20 approach plane above which no obstructions are permitted.)

In the above definitions we included two new terms: stopway and clearway. These are defined as follows:

Stopway is defined as a rectangular area, commencing at the end of the take-off run available, which is suitable for the ground run of an aeroplane decelerating after a discontinued take-off.

Clearway is defined as a rectangular area, commencing at the end of the take-off run available, selected and prepared as a suitable area over which an aircraft may make a portion of its initial climb to a specified screen height.

The general provisions of aeroplanes' weight and performance are given in Air Navigation (General) Regulations – Regulation 5.

Taxiway marking

The holding position at a runway entry point is indicated by a 4-line marking. (See Fig. 6.2a.) If it is necessary to provide separate visual and instrument taxi-holding positions, Fig. 6.2a will be used nearest to the runway, while 'ladder-style' marking (Fig. 6.2b) will be used at points further from the runway. These markings accord with amended Annex 14.

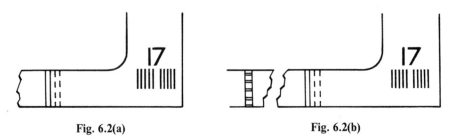

Fig. 6.2(a)   Fig. 6.2(b)

*Runway markings at CAA aerodromes

(1) All runways have a centreline, threshold and runway designation markings. (See Fig. 6.3.)

(2) Threshold markings are displaced up wind when there are obstructions present. Such displacement is indicated in Fig. 6.4.

(3) All non-instrument runways more than 1100 m in length and without VASIS, and all instrument runways, have an additional marking called 'Fixed Distance Marking' at 300 m from the threshold. (See Fig. 6.5.)

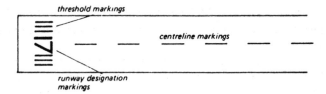

Fig. 6.3

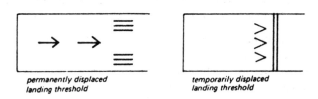

Fig. 6.4

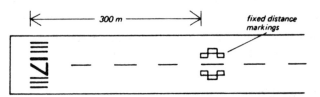

Fig. 6.5

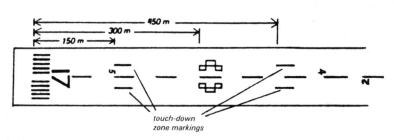

Fig. 6.6

(4) On precision approach runways, Touch-down Zone Markings up to a distance of at least 600 m are provided. These markings are placed 150 m apart. (See Fig. 6.6.)

Approach lighting

The installations serving a particular aerodrome's runways are detailed in the AGA section of the AIP. They can vary from rudimentary paraffin flares called 'goosenecks' to such high intensity runway lights that a pilot can ask ATC for them to be adjusted down if they are dazzling. Apart from judging the approach path from the perspective aspect of the runway lights, cross-bar lights etc., pilots also have visual slope guidance from approach indicators.

(1) Visual approach slope indicators (VASI)

These are of the 2-colour type and arranged as 2 pairs of white/red wingbars extending outboard of the runway. The settings are arranged to indicate (Fig. 6.7):

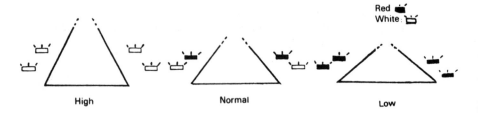

Fig. 6.7   VASI.

(a) high approach – all bars white;
(b) normal approach – near bars white, far bars red;
(c) low approach – all bars red.

(2) 3-Bar VASIS

Introduced to meet the needs of very large aircraft which have a significant difference in height between the pilot's eye level and the undercarriage, say over 15 feet. The settings are arranged to indicate:

(a) Normal aircraft. (See Fig. 6.8.)

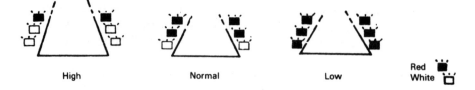

Fig. 6.8   3-Bar VASI.

(b) Aircraft with large eye/wheel characteristics. (See Fig. 6.9.)

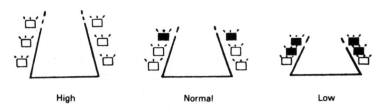

Fig. 6.9   3-Bar VASI aircraft with large eye/wheel characteristics.

(3) Low intensity 2-colour approach slope system (LITAS)

Basically similar to VASIS but with lower intensity lights and installed singly in the upwind and downwind VASIS wingbar positions, generally only on the left hand side of the runway. Indications are as VASIS.

(4) Precision approach path indicator (PAPI)

A development of VASIS with a sharper transition between red and white and a different arrangement of the lights. (See Fig. 6.10.)

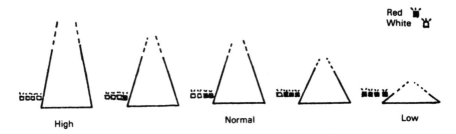

Fig. 6.10   PAPI.

MEHT (Minimum Pilot Eye Height over the Threshold) is a notified (in AGA) reference value, being the lowest height over the runway threshold of the onslope indication.

Runway visual range (RVR)

At certain aerodromes (listed in RAC section of the UK AIP) a system of passing RVRs to aircraft operates when the visibility falls below 1500 m. RVR is one of the limitations on public transport aircraft, landing or taking off (see Chapter 16). RVR observations are taken on the instrument runway in use which is normally equipped with beamed high intensity runway lighting and also, as necessary, range markers.

Range markers have the advantage of being seen in certain hazy conditions when lights cannot be seen. They are triangular in shape, 6 ft long, stand 3 ft 3 ins high, painted half black half white, with the black side of the marker nearer the runway. They are placed 9 m from the runway at a distance of 500 m from each other for the first 500 m and then at a distance of 100 m.

Method of measurement

An observer positions himself 76 m away from the centreline of the runway and as close to the landing area as possible, and counts the visible lights or markers. This visibility is then converted to visibility along the runway that a landing pilot may expect when at a height of 5 m above the centreline of the threshold.

At certain major airports, fully automatic RVR assessment, with a display system available to ATS within 15 seconds from the assessment, is installed. The system is called *Instrumented Runway Visual Range* (IRVR). Its operational range extends from nil visibility to 1500 metres.

Frequency of measurement

At aerodromes having constant traffic, RVR measurements are taken every half hour or when a significant change in the visibility is observed. At aerodromes having light traffic, observation is taken 15 minutes before the aircraft's arrival time.

Limitation of the system

The RVR assessing system suffers from the following limitations:

(1) At certain aerodromes there are local limitations. For example, some runway lights may have to be switched off before taking the RVR reading, but these lights are normally available to landing aircraft.
(2) Fog is not uniformly dense and this factor may cause wrong reports.
(3) Some time must elapse between the reading and passing it to the controller, and during this time visibility might change. The point to note is that only RVR reports are available; there is no system of forecasting, and, since the visibility can alter suddenly, the RVR reports included in VHF broadcasts are not up to date.

Aeronautical ground lights

Aeronautical ground lights installed at various civil and military aerodromes are as follows:

(1) *Identification beacons (Ibn).* These exhibit a 2-letter identification code, flashing once every 12 seconds at a speed of about 6 to 8 words per minute. The colour of the beacon light is green at civil aerodromes and red at Service aerodromes.
(2) *Aerodrome beacons (Abn).* These are located on or in the vicinity of the aerodrome. These are not installed at Service aerodromes, and at civil aerodromes this type of beacon is not generally installed if an identification beacon is available. Originally the civil aerodrome beacon showed an alternating white and green light but there are relatively few of this type left, having been superseded by white flashing (strobe) lights. Only at a very few civil aerodromes will both identification and aerodrome beacons be found operating simultaneously.

At civil aerodromes, the aeronautical ground lights normally operate during conditions of bad visibility in daytime and at the discretion of the air traffic controller at night. At certain aerodromes this discretion is not granted to the controller and the beacons operate nightly from sunset to sunrise.

At Service master aerodromes, identification beacons operate continuously during the hours of darkness; at other Service aerodromes they operate nightly to meet local requirements.

Take off, climb and landing performance of light aircraft

Fairly frequently, light aircraft are involved in accidents because the pilots have not realised the performance limitations of their aeroplanes, despite the fact that the Air Navigation Order requires them to check that the aeroplane will have adequate performance for the proposed flight. A pink Information Circular draws pilots' attention to the sources of information and factors such as WAT limitations (Weight, Altitude and Temperature), wind component, surface conditions, flap setting, humidity and slope. An uphill slope increases the ground run for take-off. Guide line factor: the take-off distance will be increased by 10% for each 2% uphill slope (i.e. a factor of x 1.1). The AIC also offers guidance on factors applicable for long grass, landing downhill, etc.

SNOCLO

When an aerodrome is unusable for take-offs and landings due to heavy snow on runways or runway snow clearance, the spoken word SNOWCLO is added to the end of that aerodrome's report when broadcast on VOLMET.

7
Flight Separation, Flight Planning, Carriage of Radio Equipment

The internationally agreed procedures are specified basically in the Procedures for Navigation Services – Rules of the Air and Air Traffic Services (PANS-RAC) and are complementary to the Standards and Recommended Practices of Annex 2 – Rules of the Air and Annex 11 – Air Traffic Services. They are also supplemented when necessary by the regional procedures contained in the Regional Supplementary Procedures (DOC 7030).

Flight separation

In order to prevent mid-air collisions the ATC provides separations to the aircraft under control. There are four types of separations as shown in Fig. 7.1 and generally an aircraft is provided with any one of these four types.

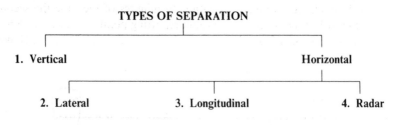

Fig. 7.1

(1) Vertical separation

This is provided by allocating different flight levels to two aircraft on reciprocal tracks. The minimum separation is 1000 ft up to 29 000 ft and 2000 ft thereafter. Vertical separation is also provided between a holding aircraft and an aircraft en route when that en route aircraft is 5 minutes flying time away.

(2) Lateral separation

Lateral separation is provided in one of two ways:

(1) *Track separation.* Track separation exists when two aircraft are flying in the following circumstances:
   (a) VOR Tracks – at least 15 degrees and at a distance of 15 nm or more from the facility.

(b) NDB Tracks – at least 30 degrees and a distance of 15 nm or more from the facility.

(c) DR – tracks diverging by at least 45 degrees and at a distance of 15 nm or more from the point of intersection of the tracks, this point being determined either visually or by reference to a navigational aid.

(2) *Geographical separation.* This is based on aircrafts' position reports.

(3) Longitudinal separation

This is the separation between aircraft in terms of the time interval between them, and is achieved in three ways: by requiring aircraft to depart at specified time, to lose time in order to arrive over a reporting point at a given time, or to hold until a specified time.

The time minima are as follows:

(1) *Aircraft flying on the same track and at the same level:*
    (a) When the preceding aircraft's speed is at least 40 knots more than the succeeding aircraft..2 min
    (b) When the preceding aircraft is at least 20 knots faster than the succeeding aircraft..5 min
    (c) In rapid fixing areas ....10 min

(2) *Aircraft crossing tracks at the same level in rapid fixing areas*............10 min

(3) *Aircraft climbing or descending through another aircraft's track:*
    (a) If level change commences within 10 minutes of the time the second aircraft has reported over an exact reporting point........................5 min
    (b) In rapid fixing areas..10 min
    (See Fig. 7.2.)

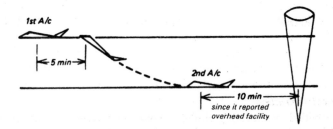

Fig. 7.2

(4) *Aircraft climbing and descending on reciprocal tracks,* vertical separation is provided (where lateral separation is not provided) from 10 min before to 10 min after the aircraft are estimated to pass.

(5) *Departing aircraft:*
    (a) If lateral separation is provided immediately on take-off..............1 min
    This time may be reduced with CAA's approval if the take-off is on parallel or non-converging runways.
    (b) Where both aircraft wish to follow the same track and when the

preceding aircraft is at least 40 knots faster than the succeeding aircraft ....2 min

(c) If after the first reporting point (in or near CTR/TMA boundary) the aircraft tracks diverge by 30°, or vertical separation is provided, the separation, with CAA approval is..5 min

(4) Radar separation

This is obtained by allocating different tracks, determined by radar. The separation minima are:

(1) 5 nm horizontal separation. This may reduce to:
(2) 3 nm when the aircraft is within 40 nm of the radar head and below flight level 245, with CAA approval;
(3) 8 nm where only SSR is available.

Flow Management

Measures have had to be introduced for those parts of the ATC system for which demand is forecast to exceed the available capacity and where ignoring the situation could well jeopardise air safety. Within the ICAO (EUR) Region, an integrated Air Traffic Flow Management (ATFM) Service optimises the use of the air traffic system by a Central Traffic Management Organisation (CTMO), with 2 Central Executive Units (CEU), West (Brussels) and East (Moscow), operating independently but interdependently.

CEU (West) is responsible for all ATFM in the airspace of the European Civil Aviation Conference (ECAC), except Iceland. Initially its functions relevant to the British Isles and the Shanwick Oceanic Control Area (OCA) are handled by the London Flight Management Unit (FMU) and details of routes to which flow regulation applies are given in the AIP together with the relevant procedure.

If a pilot wishes to fly a route subject to ATFM he must get an Approved Departure Time (ADT) from the Flow Regulator. Without an ADT, ATC will withhold departure clearance until an ADT has been obtained. When flying out of a small aerodrome outside controlled airspace and requesting joining clearance when airborne, the pilot will not get clearance without an ADT. The 'full to capacity' state may be applicable to the later stages of a flight, so even if already flying on an airway, a pilot without an ADT may well find an adjacent ATC authority refusing permission to enter its airspace.

Flight planning

A *Flight plan* is a message prepared by the pilot on a standard form and handed in to the ATC for transmission to the organisations concerned with the flight and for obtaining a clearance for the flight to proceed. It contains a wealth of information relevant to the flight such as the callsign, estimated time of departure, route details and times between reporting points, altitudes or flight levels between reporting points, true airspeed of the aircraft, radio frequencies carried, survival equipment on board and the like.

(1) When to file a flight plan?

(a) A pilot *may file* a flight plan for any flight, irrespective of whether it is IFR or VFR, inside controlled airspace or outside.

(b) A pilot *must file* a flight plan:

  (i)   For all flights within Class A Airspace.
  (ii)   When the flight takes place in controlled airspace in IMC or at night excluding SFVR.
  (iii) When a pilot elects to conduct a flight in IFR in controlled airspace when he could have flown VFR.
  (iv)   For all flights in Class D Control Zones/Control Areas irrespective of weather conditions.
  (v)   If the pilot on an advisory route wishes to use advisory service, a flight plan must be filed in spite of the fact that the advisory airspace is not controlled airspace.
  (vi)   When a pilot on special VFR wishes the destination aerodrome to be informed of his movements.
  (vii) For any flight to or from the UK which will cross the UK FIR boundary.
  (viii) For all flights within the Scottish and London Upper FIRs.
  (ix)   For any flight from a UK aerodrome to a destination more than 40 km away when the maximum total weight authorised exceeds 5700 kg.

(c) A pilot is *advised to file* a flight plan:

  (i)   When planning a flight that is likely to go beyond 10 nm of the UK coast.
  (ii)   When the flight is made over sparsely populated or mountainous areas, where Search and Rescue operations would be difficult.

(2) How to file a flight plan

You may file the flight plan at the departure aerodrome. In this case complete the form CA 48 in triplicate at least 30 min before clearance for start up or taxi is requested, and hand it in at the local Air Traffic Control. One copy is retained by the controller, the middle copy goes to the teleprinter operator and the bottom copy is handed back to you with the controller's signature for your record.

It is most important that the Flight Plan Form is correctly completed to ensure that it can be handled under the automatic data processing system. Failure to do so may well result in a delayed flight. Full instructions on the completion of flight plans are given in a yellow AIC. For operations across the North Atlantic Ocean, specific requirements apply. These vary depending on whether flights are north/south or on a Polar Track structure or south of 70°N or north of 70°N.

If the aerodrome of departure is not connected to AFTN, the pilot may telephone the flight plan to the parent unit. In this case arrangements must be made for the take-off time and airborne time to be passed subsequently to the same unit.

As much notice as possible should be given when filing a flight plan. It should be at least an hour if Controlled Airspace, Advisory Airspace etc., is involved and at least 30 min before clearance to taxi for other flights.

Alternatively, a pilot may file a flight plan while airborne. The message must commence with the sentence 'I wish to file an airborne flight plan,' and be addressed to the FIR controller or, failing that, to any Air Traffic Service unit. Generally, airborne flight plans are filed when it is decided to enter a controlled airspace which was not originally planned. In this case you must file the plan at least 10 min before the entry is required. Another alternative is to file an Abbreviated Flight Plan just for clearance for a limited portion of a flight.

*(3) Addressing of flight plans
(a) Both the flight plan and subsequent flight plan messages will be addressed by the ATSU where the departure aerodrome is on AFTN.

(b) Where the aerodrome is not on the AFTN, the pilot should pass the flight plan to a licensed ATS unit and address the flight plan to:
   (i)   destination aerodrome;
   (ii) all ATCCs through which the flight will pass;
   (iii) up to two operators' addresses, but three addresses if one is on the destination airfield.

(c) Flight plans are delivered only to those on AFTN, or linked to it by a parent unit. If a flight is to any other aerodrome the pilot should notify the intended flight to his destination by private arrangement.

*(4) Messages
After the filing of a flight plan, the following routine messages are sent to the same addresses as on the flight plan, as appropriate:

(a) *Departure.* The message takes the following form:

Type	Callsign	Time Group
DEP	G – ABCD	2110

(The present policy is to phase out DEP messages.)

(b) *Delay.* This message is sent when the aircraft is delayed by 30 min or more:

Type	Callsign	Revised ETD
DLA	G – ABCD	2205

(c) *Cancellation.* This is sent out if the flight is cancelled after a flight plan has been filed:

Type	Callsign
CNL	G – ABCD

(d) *Arrival message.* This is sent in two instances:
   (i)   When an aircraft lands at an aerodrome other than the aerodrome shown in the flight plan as destination. On arrival, the message is sent to all ACC/FIRs through which the aircraft would have passed according to the flight plan.

(ii) When an aircraft lands after having experienced radio failure. The message takes the following form:

Type	Callsign	Aerodrome Landed	Time of Arrival
ARR	G – ABCD	EGPO	0420

(e) *Modification.* This message is sent whenever any data contained in the flight plan are altered. It takes the following form:

Type	CHG	Callsign	Item No.	Amendment

(f) *Supplementary flight plan message (SPL).* This message is initiated by an aircraft's departure aerodrome or parent ATCC in response to a 'request information' (RQ) message from the flight's destination aerodrome or other authority who wishes to know the number of passengers that were carried on that aircraft. Normally this information is held by the operator/handling agency at the departure aerodrome. If the operator/handling authority closes down before a flight's ETA plus one hour at the destination, this information is passed to the aerodrome ATS unit. If this unit closes down before the flight's ETA plus one hour to destination, it, in its turn, passes this information to the parent ATCC.

(g) *Repetitive flight plans (RFP).* These apply to frequently recurring, regularly operated IFR flights with identical Basic features. Submitted by an operator to ATS Units for storage and repetitive use for individual flights, it offers operators and ATS Units considerable advantages in handling flight plan data. An RFP may be filed subject to:
(i)   having a high degree of stability;
(ii) flights must be operated at the same time(s) of the day, on the same days of consecutive weeks and on at least 10 occasions, unchanged;
(iii) it must cover the entire flight from the departure aerodrome to the aerodrome of first intended landing;
(iv) all ATS units involved must agree.

(5) Deviation

If the pilot decides to land elsewhere he must inform the ATCC/FIR as soon as possible, subsequently giving details of the new route. In any case, he must inform the original destination within 30 min of his ETA there, as otherwise a search operation would be initiated.

(6) Cancellation of IFR

A pilot may request cancellation of an IFR flight plan when in the controlled airspace, provided he can maintain VMC and provided the controlled airspace concerned is not notified as Class A Airspace. The message for this purpose is 'Callsign, cancel IFR flight plan'. ATC cannot approve or disapprove such a request; they will, however, advise the pilot if he is likely to meet with IMC later in the flight. A mere report that a pilot is VMC does not constitute cancellation of the flight plan. Remember the conditions for which filing a flight plan is mandatory.

(7) Booking in and out

Every pilot undertaking a flight is required to 'book out' at the aerodrome ATS unit. A booking out does not constitute filing a flight plan; but, when a flight plan is filed, a separate booking out is not required. Similarly, a pilot who has just made a flight is required to 'book in' at the ATS unit.

*Carriage of radio equipment

The following communication and navigation equipment is prescribed by the ANO for all aircraft flying in the type of airspace stated.

(1) Communication equipment

VHF RTF with appropriate ATC frequencies when flying in controlled airspace notified for the purposes of ANO Schedule 5; under IFR in Controlled Airspace below FL 245; flight in Upper Airspace (i.e. at or above FL 245), except gliders.

(2) Navigation equipment

Under IFR in controlled airspace notified for the purposes of ANO schedule 5; under IFR in Controlled Airspace below FL 245; flight in Upper Airspace (except gliders). Either VOR, DME and ADF or Decca and Flight Log. (Aircraft cleared for a special VFR are exempt from this requirement.)

(3) Approach aids

An approach aid (e.g. ILS) must be carried if landing at specified aerodromes within the CTR. Details are to be found in the AGA section of the UK AIP.

(4) Public transport

In addition to the above, aircraft flying for public transport purposes must carry a 75 MHz marker beacon receiver and the following equipment:

(a) When IFR:
  (i) appropriate radio frequencies to be able to receive meteorological broadcasts;
  (ii) A suitable receiver to receive signals from the ground to guide the pilot down to a point from which visual landing can be made.
(b) When VFR:
  (i) When over land and navigation is not carried out by reference to the earth's surface, aircraft must carry equipment of a type approved by the CAA which will enable the aircraft to maintain two-way communication with the appropriate ATC unit and at the same time to be navigated in accordance with its flight plan and ATC instructions.
  (ii) When over water beyond gliding distance of any land, equipment to maintain two-way communication with the appropriate ATC unit must be carried.

(5) Secondary surveillance radar

All aircraft in the UK when flying under IFR within controlled airspace notified for the purposes of ANO Schedule 5 and (other than gliders) when flying at and above FL 100 and/or when flying within airspace notified for the purposes of this sub-paragraph as having special rules prescribed *must* carry SSR transponder equipment having a Mode A-4096 code and Mode C with altitude reporting capability. A transponder having a Mode A-4096 code capability is required in Scottish TMA above 6000 feet *altitude* at all times. SSR having a Mode A-4096 code and Mode C with altitude reporting capability must be carried in *all* UK airspace at and above FL 100.

The requirement to carry SSR transponders does not apply to:

(a) Gliders.
(b) Aircraft below FL 100 in controlled airspace receiving an approved crossing service.

Action in the event of radio failure

If you are instructed by ATC to change frequency to contact another control and you are unable to establish two-way communication, revert to the previous frequency and tell ATC of the failure. For other situations, there are laid down procedures.

Failure of radio navigation aids

In the event of failure of radio navigation aids, adopt the following procedure:

(1) Report the failure to ATC, giving altitude and approximate position.
(2) ATC may give permission to continue the flight in, or into, controlled airspace. Radar may help in navigation.
(3) If no permission is given:
   (a) leave or avoid the controlled airspace and areas of dense traffic;
   (b) proceed to VMC area and continue the flight in VMC. If this is not possible, then:
   (c) break cloud in a suitable area, proceed VMC to a suitable aerodrome and land as soon as practicable.
(4) Take advice from ATC.
(5) Make full use of ground DF, and:
(6) Keep ATC informed of intentions at all times.

Failure of SSR transponder

(1) SSR plays such an important part in ATS that accommodation of an aircraft without a serviceable transponder is becoming increasingly difficult.
(2) If the transponder fails before departure and cannot be repaired:
   (a) Go to the nearest aerodrome where it can be repaired.
   (b) Inform ATS preferably before submission of a flight plan. Clearance may then be granted, though perhaps with a modified departure time, F/L or route, depending on existing or anticipated traffic.

   (c) Insert the letter N under SSR for complete or partial failure on ICAO
        flight plan.
(3) If the transponder fails en route, ATS will try to continue the flight as
     planned, or the aircraft will be ordered to return to departure aerodrome or
     land at another mutually acceptable aerodrome. If the transponder cannot
     be repaired then, the provisions of paragraph 2 apply. It is all very tough.

At present temporary failure of SSR Mode C alone would not restrict the normal
operation of the flight.

Failure of communication radio

In the event of failure of *communication* radio in controlled airspace, the
procedures are slightly complicated. The basic procedure is to continue the flight
in accordance with the current flight plan to the holding point at the aerodrome
of first intended landing. Operate the SSR transponder on mode A code 7600
with mode C. If the aircraft's transmitter is thought still to be serviceable,
continue to transmit position reports at appropriate times on appropriate
frequencies.

   The best way to familiarise oneself with the procedures is to take a
hypothetical flight, and follow it through the different flight stages. Let us plan
a flight from A to E at FL 160. En route reporting points are B and C, and D is
the first IFR facility for the destination, E. It is planned to climb to the cruising
level immediately on take-off. At reporting point C, it is planned to descend to
FL 120 and the final descent for landing is to start at D. With the take-off at 1000
hrs the flight plan ETAs to various reporting points are shown on Fig. 7.3.

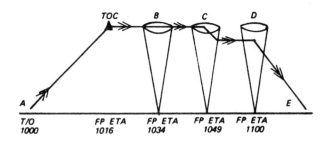

Fig. 7.3

Climb phase

You may be lucky and receive a clearance to take-off and climb directly to FL
160. If you are given such a clearance and the radio communication fails during
the climb, your action is to continue to climb to the cleared flight level and then
proceed according to your flight plan.

   The chances are that your clearance will read something like this: 'Cleared to
E via Romeo 3, climb to FL 80 and request level change en route to FL 180'. This
type of clearance is called RLCE (Request Level Change En route) clearance and

it means that you may climb to FL 80 and that, on arrival at that flight level, you will be assigned FL 180 as cruising level. In the event of radio failure before FL 80 is reached, your action is as follows:

(1) Proceed in accordance with the clearance, climbing to the assigned level (FL 80 in our illustration).
(2) Then turn left or right 60° and leave the controlled airspace.
(3) When clear of the controlled airspace, climb to planned level, FL 160 in our case (and not FL 180 which you expected would be assigned had the radio been serviceable).
(4) Keep clear of the controlled airspace for at least 5 min.
(5) Rejoin the controlled airspace.
(6) If the flight is departing for a foreign FIR the climb must be completed before leaving UK FIR.

On occasions, the ATC, having once cleared an aircraft to a level, may subsequently find it necessary to restrict its climb. If the communication fails during this phase of the climb, the appropriate action is as per RLCE clearance described above.

Most of the busy aerodromes nowadays have Standard Instrument Departure (SID) procedures, which may or may not represent Noise Abatement Procedures (NAPs). On such departures, allotted tracks are strictly to be adhered to and for the purpose of noise abatement, crossing altitudes will also be given in the clearance. On most occasions where radar is available, the climb takes place under radar supervision. With instruction to climb under radar a typical clearance may read something like this: 'Cleared to E via Golf One (and if A is Heathrow and the take-off is on R/W 09L), turn right after passing the end of the runway and proceed to WOODLEY. Climb to 3000 ft and maintain until west of 215° R VOR LON then cross WOODLEY NDB at 4000 ft'.

If the communication fails at any stage during the above procedure, your action is to follow the instructions up to WOODLEY NDB. After WOODLEY climb on track to the flight plan flight level. You are under radar and therefore there is no need for you temporarily to leave the controlled airspace to achieve the requested flight level.

En route phase

In the event of communication failure the following *basic procedures* are prescribed.

(1) Maintain last acknowledged cruising level to the point cleared, and then revert to the flight level requested in the flight plan. Thus, in the present illustration, if the radio failure had not occurred during the climb, you would be cruising at FL 180, and the clearance would probably extend to reporting point C. If so, you must maintain FL 180 until C or any other reporting point to which you have been cleared at that flight level.

If you had been assigned FL 180 up to reporting point B, you would maintain that flight level up to B. At B you would revert to the flight plan flight level, that is, FL 160. Further, when you arrive at C, you would descend to FL 120 as planned.

(2) As for the timing during this phase of the flight, your main requirement is to arrive at the holding point (that is, facility D) as close to the ETA as possible. The ETA is worked out in the following manner:

    (a) If you had transmitted your ETA to D and this was acknowledged by the ATC, then this is the ETA.

    (b) If no such ETA has been acknowledged, then compute your ETA to D by going back to the last acknowledged ETA and using flight plan times from there on. Say, you arrived at B at 1032 and with your position report you passed your ETA to C as 1046. This was acknowledged and the radio failure occurs between B and C. Your ETA to D is then 1046 + 11 min (flight plan time) = 1057. You should then endeavour to arrive at D at this time since the ATC will be working on this figure.

(3) Follow the standard routes and if the transmitter is thought to be working, send requisite position reports.

(4) Operate secondary transponder radar on mode A, code 7600 with mode C.

Descent phase

Now, it is quite possible that the radio was serviceable until just before arriving at the holding point D. In that case you would have passed your ETA either to the destination or the zone, and in return you would have received one of the three messages: 'No Delay Expected,' 'Delay Not Determined' or 'Estimated Approach Time (EAT) . . .'. It is equally possible that you have been a mute aircraft for a considerable time and you are arriving over the holding point on an ETA worked out as above. The meaning of the above three messages and the rules of descent are as follows:

(1) *No delay expected.* The meaning of this message is obvious – you expect to be given clearance to descend on your arrival at D, the holding point (or the first facility). In case of communication failure after receiving this message and also if you are arriving after a long period of radio silence (and therefore, not having received any messages) your action is to plan to arrive as close to the ETA as possible at your flight plan flight level. Commence your descent, at the earliest on your ETA, and at the latest, ETA + 10 min. In our illustration the descent must be commenced between 1057 and 1107. The rate of descent must not be less than 500 ft/min.

(2) *Delay not determined.* If this is the last message received before radio failure occurs, you are not permitted to land at your planned destination: you must divert.

(3) *Expected approach time – EAT.* EAT is the time at which the ATC unit concerned expects that an arriving aircraft will be cleared to leave the lowest level of the holding stack to start approach for landing. EAT is based on the actual traffic situation and is passed to arriving aircraft only when they will be required to hold. EAT is therefore your ETA as far as the descent is

concerned. Commence your descent on EAT earliest, EAT + 10 min latest, the rate of descent still being not less than 500 ft/min. In the UK, ATCCs will not issue EATs when the terminal area delay is likely to be less than 20 min. Additional procedures for issuing EATs apply for Heathrow and Gatwick.

Landing phase and diversion

The descent should commence on EAT or ETA as explained above. You are allowed a time tolerance of 10 min if you could not commence descent on ETA/EAT. Irrespective of what time you commenced your descent, you must land within 30 min of the time the descent should have commenced, that is, ETA/EAT + 30. If you cannot do this then:

(1) If it is possible to remain VMC, stay in the circuit and make further attempts at approach and landing visually.
(2) If you are not VMC, or if you have arrived over the holding point after receiving 'Delay Not Determined' message, leave the aerodrome vicinity and the controlled airspace at the specified altitude along the specified route where this is prescribed in RAC Section of the UK AIP. If altitude or route is not specified, fly at the last assigned altitude or minimum sector altitude, whichever is higher, and avoid dense traffic. Then fly either to an area where you can become VMC and land there, or break cloud in a suitable area and land as soon as possible. In either case inform ATC on landing.

(*Note:* In our illustration above we have taken FL 120 as the arrival flight level at the first facility D. Normally you would flight plan to arrive overhead D at the published altitude so that you could commence descent for approach and landing directly on arrival overhead. A higher flight level assigned by the ATC holding would be expected.)

Procedures in various circumstances

In addition to the above basic procedures, procedures appropriate to particular circumstances have also been prescribed. These are as follows.

If flight can be maintained under VMC, continue and land at a suitable airfield. Report to ATC by the most expeditious means. If flight cannot be maintained under VMC, adopt one of the following IMC procedures as appropriate.

IMC Procedures

---

(1) A flight is planned to enter controlled airspace, or it is taking place within controlled airspace, the navigation equipment is functioning and the pilot is properly qualified.

(a) If a flight plan has been filed and the clearance has been received and acknowledged

or

communication has been established

and

airborne flight plan has been filed and a request for clearance had been made

and

both these have been acknowledged.

Adopt basic procedures

(b) No clearance or communication has been received, or a message received from the destination aerodrome saying 'Delay not determined' and radio failure occurred after that

Leave or avoid controlled airspace. Either fly to VMC area and continue in VMC, or break cloud and proceed visually and land as soon as possible. Inform ATCC on landing.

---

(2) Aircraft is taking off from a CTR and navigation equipment is functioning properly:

(a) Radio failure occurs after being cleared by approach control to communicate with ATCC.

Adopt basic procedures

(b) Radio failure occurred before such clearance to change over to ATCC frequency was received.

Return visually to aerodrome of departure. If this is not practicable leave controlled airspace and adopt basic procedure or adopt basic procedure described in 1(b) above.

(c) Radio failure occurs after 'RLCE-type' or radar-type clearance received and cleared to communicate with ATCC.

Adopt procedure given under 'Climb Phase' section earlier in this chapter

---

(3) There is an emergency and it is necessary to cross an airway

Cross at intermediate levels of 500 ft

---

(4) Navigation equipment is inadequate to follow the flight plan

Follow procedure in 1(b) above.

---

(5) Flight is not planned to enter controlled airspace or it is not taking place within controlled airspace

Follow procedure in 1(b) above.

(6) During a Radar Approach, if communication fails prior to final approach	Continue approach visually or using available aids; if this is not possible proceed to the holding point at last assigned altitude or published missed approach altitude (whichever is higher) and adopt basic procedure.
(7) During a radar approach, if communication fails on the final approach.	Continue approach visually or using available aids; if this is not possible, adopt published missed approach procedure then basic procedures.

A last resort

As a last resort, a pink AIC tells pilots that 'for many years, Military Flight Information Publications have published a procedure designed to attract help in cases where radio failure is compounded by uncertainty of position'.

The procedure is to fly the 'emergency triangle' and it really is a last resort, only to be used under actual conditions.

(1) Switch SSR to emergency code and continue to try to make radio contact, listening out on appropriate emergency frequency.
(2) Maintain sufficient altitude both to ensure safe clearance of terrain and of any suspected obstacles and also to improve the chances of the aircraft being seen on ground radar.
(3) Fly a triangular route making the 120° turns as tight as practicable, with two minute legs if TAS is less than 300 kt and of one minute legs if TAS is over 300 kt.
(4) If only the receiver is serviceable fly the triangular pattern by making the turns to the right (Fig. 7.4), while if both the receiver and the transmitter are unserviceable fly the triangular pattern to the left (Fig. 7.5).

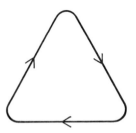

Fig. 7.4 Only receiver operating.

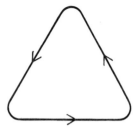

Fig. 7.5 Both receiver and transmitter unserviceable.

When the ground authority sees the triangular pattern being flown, it will try to contact the aircraft on the appropriate emergency frequency and inform the relevant ATC authority. Whenever possible the aircraft should be flying in VMC and flying at the best height for endurance. A 'shepherd' aircraft will intercept the distressed aircraft. The distressed aircraft will formate in echelon on the 'shepherd' and will be led to an aerodrome to make visual contact.

8
Flight at Aerodromes

The international legislation relating to aerodromes is set out in Annex 14. An aerodrome is defined as any area of land or water designed, equipped, set apart, or commonly used to afford facilities for the take-off and landing of aircraft, and includes any area or space, whether on the ground, on the roof of a building or elsewhere, which is designed, equipped or set apart for affording facilities for the landing and departure of aircraft capable of descending or climbing vertically.

For the following aerodromes during the times given, airspaces (notified for the purposes of the Rules of the Air Regulations) called *Aerodrome Traffic Zones* (ATZs) are specified with standard dimensions of:

(1) for an off-shore installation, from mean sea level to 2000 ft amsl and within a radius of 1.5 nm of the installation;
(2) for a non-offshore installation, an extent depending upon the length of the longest runway.
   (a) If the longest runway is notified as 1850 m or less, it is the airspace extending from the surface to a height of 2000 ft above aerodrome level within the area bounded by a circle of 2 nm radius centred on the notified mid-point of the longest runway. (If, because of the runway pattern at the aerodrome, such an ATZ would not extend 1.5 nm beyond the end of any runway then the following rule (b) applies.)
   (b) If the longest runway is notified as greater than 1850 metres, it is the airspace from the surface to 2000 ft above aerodrome level within the area bounded by a circle of 2.5 nm centred on the notified mid-point of the longest runway.

All this is 'except for any part of the ATZ which is within the ATZ of another aerodrome which has been notified as being the "controlling aerodrome"'.

ATZs are not allocated specific class of Airspace. They adopt the class of Airspace within which they are located, which may vary from Class A to Class G. *The Rules of the Air Regulations* notify operational procedures for the ATZs of the aerodromes tabulated.

Aerodrome	Hours
(1) A government aerodrome	Such times as are notified
(2) An aerodrome having an air traffic control unit or an aerodrome flight information unit	During the notified hours of watch of the air traffic control unit or the aerodrome flight information unit

(3) A licensed aerodrome having a
    means of two-way radio
    communication with aircraft

During the notified hours of watch
of the air/ground radio station

For these aerodromes, an aircraft cannot fly, take off or land within the ATZ
unless the pilot has obtained permission from the aerodrome's ATC or if the
aerodrome has no ATC, from the Aerodrome's Flight Information Unit enough
information as to enable safe flight within the ATZ. If there is neither ATC nor
Flight Information Unit the pilot has to obtain information from the air/ground
radio station to enable safe flight to be made in the ATZ.

When flying in an ATZ a pilot must:

(1) listen out continuously on the notified radio frequency for the aerodrome
    and if he has no radio, keep watch for visual signals;
(2) if he has radio, notify his position and height to the aerodrome on entering
    and when about to leave its ATZ.

There are special rules for the notified airspace Upper Heyford Mandatory Rules
Area which is accorded its own Rule in the Rules of the Air Regulations.

At certain military aerodromes, Military Aerodrome Traffic Zones (MATZ)
are established to provide increased protection to aircraft flying within their
airspace. The main portion of a MATZ comprises the airspace within 5 nm of the
mid-point of its longest runway, from the surface to 3000 ft above aerodrome
level. Projecting from this airspace is a stub, aligned with a selected final
approach path. Its length is 5 nm along its centreline, width 4 nm (that is, 2 nm
either side of the centreline) extending vertically from 1000 ft above aerodrome
level to 3000 ft above aerodrome level. (This stub may be absent or reduced in
size at some aerodromes while others may have two stubs.) There are some local
variations from these usual dimensions.

A large proportion of these MATZ participate in what is known as a
penetration scheme for civil aircraft. This is available during the normal hours of
watch of the ATC units. The procedures for penetrating a MATZ are as follows:

(1) Call the controlling aerodrome when 15 nm or 5 min flying time from the
    zone   boundary,   whichever   is   the   greater,   using   phraseology
    '. . . (Controlling Aerodrome), this is . . . (aircraft call-sign), request MATZ
    penetration'.
(2) When two-way communication is established and the controller asks you to
    go ahead, pass further information: call-sign, type of aircraft, position,
    heading, altitude, intentions (e.g. destination).
(3) Comply with instructions while in the MATZ, maintain listening watch on
    the allocated RTF frequency and advise the controller when clear of the
    MATZ.

The controller will provide radar separation if radar is available, otherwise a
vertical separation of at least 500 ft will be used. The altimeter setting given will

be the aerodrome QNH. (RN aerodromes will give QFE.) Where two MATZ are combined the lower aerodrome QNH of the aerodromes will be passed as 'clutch QNH'.

Always call the MATZ controller when at the regulation distance even if you consider that you are outside normal watch hours because the aerodrome may be operational serving night flying. If no reply is received to two consecutive calls it may be assumed that the aerodrome is closed but proceed with caution. Lastly, separation is provided between aircraft complying with these procedures. Since these procedures are not compulsory, keep a careful lookout at all times. Pilots are also responsible for terrain clearance.

Aerodrome signals and markings

Aerodromes have various means of communicating with aircraft without radio by means of visual signals, and aircraft with radio may also take advantage of them. These standard signals are displayed in a 'signals area' near the air traffic building and the symbolic figures have assigned meanings. Signals normally seen at an aerodrome are given below.

(1) *Direction of landing.* A white T displayed in the signals area indicates the direction of landing. Landing direction is parallel to the shaft of the T and towards the cross arm. (Fig. 8.1.)
(2) *Prohibition of landing.* This is indicated by means of a red square panel with yellow diagonals. (Fig. 8.2.)
(3) *Special precautions.* A red square panel with a single yellow diagonal only, signifies that the state of the manoeuvring area is poor and that pilots must exercise special care when landing. (Fig. 8.3.)
(4) *Use hard surface only.* This is indicated by a white dumb-bell. (Fig. 8.4.)
(5) *Take-off and land on the runway, ground movement not confined to hard surface.* This is indicated by a black strip on each circular portion of the dumb-bell, at right angles to the shaft. (Fig. 8.5.)

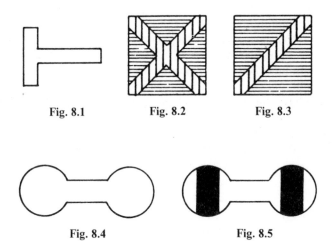

Fig. 8.1   Fig. 8.2   Fig. 8.3

Fig. 8.4   Fig. 8.5

(6) *Direction of take-off and landing not necessarily the same.* This is indicated in two ways: a black ball suspended from a mast, and a white disc placed along the cross arm of the T. (Fig. 8.6.)

(7) *Right hand circuit in progress.* This is indicated by a red and yellow striped arrow pointing in a clockwise direction; also a green flag may be flown from a mast. (Fig. 8.7.)

(8) *Glider-flying in progress.* Signified by a double white cross and/or two red balls suspended from a mast. A yellow cross indictes the tow-rope dropping area. (Fig. 8.8.)

(9) *Helicopter operations.* Where helicopters are required to take-off and land only within a designated area, a white letter H is displayed in the signals area. Another letter H, considerably larger in dimensions, indicates the area to be used by helicopters.

(10) *Landing area for light aircraft.* A white letter L indicates a part of the manoeuvring area which shall be used only for the taking off and landing of light aircraft. A red letter L displayed on the dumb-bell signifies that light aircraft are permitted to take-off and land either on a runway or on the area designated by the white letter L.

(11) *Runway indication.* This is given by black numerals in two-figure groups, e.g. 24, which means that the magnetic direction of the runway in use is 240°.

(12) *Aerodrome Control in Operation.* A checkered flag or board containing 12 equal squares, coloured red and yellow alternately, signifies that the aircraft may move on the manoeuvring area and apron only in accordance with the permission of the air traffic control unit at the aerodrome. (Fig. 8.9.)

(13) *Reporting point.* A black letter C against a yellow background indicates the position where a pilot can report to the air traffic control unit. This point need not necessarily be located at the tower building.

(14) *Unserviceable portion of runway or taxiway.* Two or more white crosses displayed on a runway/taxiway with the arms of the crosses at an angle of 45° to the centreline of the runway indicates that the portion enclosed is unserviceable. The crosses are not placed more than 300 m apart. They are visible from the air. To guide the taxiing aircraft, orange and white markers are placed not more than 45 m apart at the boundary of the unfit area.

(15) *Unserviceable portion of unpaved manoeuvring area.* This is marked off by means of triangular orange and white striped markers, alternating with flags, showing equal orange and red triangular areas. (Fig. 8.10.)

(16) *Aerodrome boundary markings.* Striped triangular markers, orange and white, placed not more than 45 m apart are used for this purpose. On structures, similar flat markers are used.

(17) *Boundary of unpaved runway or stopway.* Marked by white flat rectangular markers, flush with the surface.

(18) *Holding position.* A broken white line and a continuous white line close together across a taxiway mark the point beyond which no part of an aircraft or vehicle can project towards the runway without ATC permission.

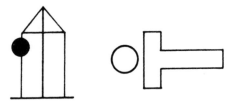

Fig. 8.6

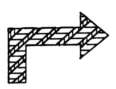 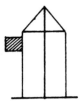

Fig. 8.7

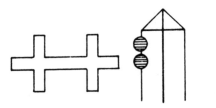

Fig. 8.8

Fig. 8.9   Fig. 8.10

In addition to above, the following signals, with which you should be familiar, may be seen at a military aerodrome:

(1) *Light aircraft.* A red L indicates that light aircraft may land on a special grass area, delineated by white markings. Taxiing on grass by such aircraft is permitted.
(2) *Landing dangerous.* Generally found at disused airfields, and indicated by a white cross. Aircraft must not make a planned landing as the airfield is used for storage purposes only.
(3) *Emergency use only.* A white cross with a white bar displayed at the end of a runway at a disused aerodrome indicates that the runway is fit for emergency use only. The Service does not provide any guarantee of safe emergency use for such runways; the indication simply signifies that the runway concerned has been inspected by the Service within the last six months and that, at the time of the inspection, it was found suitable for emergency landing.
(4) *Unserviceable areas.* These are marked off by solid orange triangles.
(5) *Carrier procedure training.* This is indicated by a white square panel with a red diamond superimposed.
(6) *Variable circuit.* If the direction of the circuit is variable, a red flag will be flown to indicate left-hand circuit and a green flag when right-hand circuit is in operation.

Table 8.1   Visual signals

Signal	Meaning to a/c on ground	Meaning to a/c in the air
(1) Green flashes	Authorises movement on the manoeuvring area and apron	Return to the circuit or remain in the circuit and await signal for permission to land
(2) Continuous green	Authorises take-off	Authorises landing
(3) Red flashes	Move clear of landing strip immediately	Owing to aerodrome being unfit for use or for any other reason, a landing should be made elsewhere
(4) Continuous red	Stop	Give way to other aircraft and continue circling
(5) White flashes	Return to your starting point	Land at this aerodrome, after receiving green light and then, after receiving green flashes, proceed to the apron
(6) Red pyro light or flare		Prohibits aircraft from landing for the time being, cancelling any previous permission to land

(7) *Land in emergency only.* Two vertical yellow bars on a red square in the signals area indicate that the landing areas are serviceable but the normal safety facilities are not available.

The pilot of an aircraft, irrespective of whether it carries radio or not, may receive instructions by means of visual light/pyrotechnic signals. These signals together with their meaning are given in Table 8.1.

Similarly, an aircraft may communicate with the ATC by means of visual light/pyro signals, as in Table 8.2.

Table 8.2 Visual communication

Signal	Meaning
(1) Red pyro light, or red flare	Immediate assistance is requested
(2) Green flashes, or continuous green light or green pyrotechnic light	By night: May I land? By day: May I land in different direction from that indicated by landing T?
(3) White flashes, or white pyro lights, or switching on and off the navigation lights, or switching on and off of landing lights	I am compelled to land

Finally, when on the route, you might have a surprise and see a series of red and green lights or stars which indicates that the aircraft is in an active danger area, restricted or prohibited area. On seeing this signal, the correct action to take is as follows:

(1) Do not penetrate any further into the restricted area and do not alter your height while in it.
(2) Get out of the area by shortest route.

The same signal is used to indicate that an aircraft is about to enter an active danger area, prohibited or restricted area and should alter course to avoid the area.

As for the regulation of traffic, the air traffic control work is shared between the Aerodrome Controller and the Approach Controller. The Aerodrome Control Service operates as follows:

(1) Departing aircraft will be given taxi instructions, altimeter setting, take-off clearance, etc.
(2) Arriving aircraft will be given their turn to land, runway in use, altimeter setting, wind velocity, obstruction, taxi instructions after landing, etc. If, however, an approach control service is operating to IFR flights, this information will be passed to the aircraft by the approach controller.

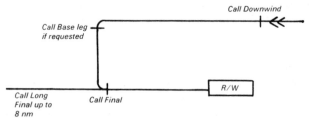

Call Downwind when abeam upwind end of the runway.

Call Base leg if requested by the ATC immediately on completion of the turn on to base leg.

Call Final after completion of the turn on to final approach and when at a range of not more than 4 nm from the approach end of the runway.

Call Long Final when making a straight-in approach, or a normal approach beyond 4 nm range, up to 8 nm. Again call Final when a range of 4 nm is reached.

Fig. 8.11

Visual circuit is carried out as shown in Fig. 8.11.

Priority of landing

The general rule is, 'first come, first land'. However, where two or more aircraft approach to land at the same time, the priority belongs to the aircraft at the lowest height. This aircraft, however, loses its priority in any of the following three circumstances:

(1) if, in order to exercise its priority, the aircraft overtakes or cuts-in in front of another aircraft which is already on finals;
(2) where the ATC unit has given out an order of priority;
(3) where another aircraft wishes to land in emergency.

In this last instance, if the incident occurs at night, the pilot who aborted his landing attempt in favour of the crippled aircraft must consider his previous permission to land as having been cancelled. He must obtain a fresh landing permission before another attempt at landing is made. Aircraft landing or on the approach to land have right of way over other aircraft in flight or on the ground.

Use of runways
(1) Normally, only one aircraft may land at a time. However, an aircraft may land before the preceding aircraft has cleared the runway if the following four conditions are satisfied:
    (a) the runway is long enough to hold both the aircraft;
    (b) during daylight only, and
    (c) the preceding aircraft is visible to the succeeding aircraft throughout the period that the other aircraft remains on the runway;
    (d) the second aircraft has been warned.
(2) In the case of two aircraft cleared to land on the same runway, the air traffic

instructions will be 'land after . . . (aircraft)' instead of 'clear to land'. It will then be the pilot's responsibility to decide how far behind the first aircraft to land.

(3) The local air traffic unit will nominate a runway for use which they consider to be the best suited to the existing circumstances. However, whether to land on that runway or another is the pilot's decision.

(4) On take-off, if the instruction received is 'cleared to immediate take-off', taxi on to the runway and commence take-off without stopping. If already on the runway, commence take-off without delay.

Closure of aerodromes

An air traffic controller may close a CAA or public-licensed aerodrome in one of the following three circumstances:

(1) when the landing area is unfit;
(2) when the closure is published in NOTAM;
(3) when essential facilities have failed. The term 'essential facilities' will be interpreted in light of existing circumstances.

An air traffic controller has no authority to close an aerodrome simply for weather reasons. Arriving aircraft receive weather information either from the VOLMET broadcasts or through ATCC or the aerodrome control, and if the destination weather is bad it is for the pilot to decide whether to continue or to divert. The first aircraft arriving at a bad weather aerodrome will be cleared to make an approach by the message 'No Delay Expected'. If this aircraft holds to wait an improvement in the weather, all other aircraft arriving subsequently will be given the message 'Delay Not Determined'. These aircraft will be assigned a level in the holding stack but any of these may request permission to attempt an approach. The controller will then pass descent and routing instructions to the pilot to clear the holding stack and he will be given his EAT. In congested terminal areas serving busy airports where short duration holding can often occur at short notice, ATCCs will not normally issue EATs to aircraft when the delay is expected to be less than 20 min.

*Approach Control service

Where an Approach Control service is established at aerodromes outside the controlled airspace (control zone, in this case) there is no legal requirement for pilots flying in IMC to obey Approach Control instructions unless flying inside the aerodrome traffic zone. This weakness in law makes such control service of only advisory value. Pilots, however, are strongly advised to avoid flying within 10 nm of the aerodromes and below 3000 ft in IFR. They are further advised that if they do fly within this area, they should inform the Approach Control 10 min before entry, and put themselves voluntarily under its control. The duties of Approach Controllers are described in the following paragraphs.

Aerodromes within Controlled Airspace
(1) Approach Control will take over inbound traffic when released by the ATCC and provide separation service until handed over to the Aerodrome Control. Similar service in reverse is provided to outbound traffic.
(2) Aircraft inbound from FIR (this term is commonly used to signify uncontrolled airspace, although technically it includes both types of airspace) come under the jurisdiction of the Approach Control on entry into the zone, until transferred to the aerodrome control.

Aerodromes outside Controlled Airspace
As pointed out above, this is an advisory service provided to aircraft under IFR, the main service being separation service to both arriving and departing aircraft.

(1) Departing aircraft cease to be under control when:
   (a) more than 10 min flying time away, or
   (b) taken over by ATCC, or
   (c) the pilot no longer wishes to be controlled, whichever of the three occurs soonest.
(2) Transit aircraft remain under control until either they are clear of the approach pattern or no longer wish to be controlled.
(3) Arriving aircraft contact Approach Control when released by ATCC or when 10 min flying time away, if outside controlled airspace. They will then receive the following information:
   (a) runway in use;
   (b) surface wind direction and speed;
   (c) visibility;
   (d) present weather;
   (e) significant cloud;
   (f) QFE or QNH (with height of aerodrome);
   (g) other information (e.g. gusts);
   (h) Runway Visual Range.

VFR contact approach
A VFR contact approach is defined as an instrument approach by an IFR flight when part or all of the procedure is completed with visual reference to the terrain. IFR flight may be authorised to do a visual contact approach to expedite traffic, provided:

(1) the pilot has the aerodrome in sight, and
(2) either the cloud ceiling is not below the initial approach level, or the pilot reports that he can complete a visual approach.

Of course, if the conditions are full VMC, the pilot may always request cancellation of IFR flight plan and make a VFR approach. On the other hand, if the conditions are IMC, he must make a full IFR approach.

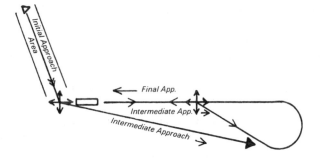

Fig. 8.12

*IFR approach
An IFR approach is carried out in three stages, that is, initial approach, intermediate approach, and final approach. These three terms are defined as follows, and the stages are shown in Fig. 8.12.

Initial Approach is that part of an instrument approach procedure consisting of the first approach to the first navigational facility associated with the procedure, or to a pre-determined fix.

The initial approach generally takes place in the 'Initial Approach Area'. This is an area of defined width lying between the last preceding navigational fix, or dead reckoning position, and the facility to be used for making an instrument approach, or a point associated with such a facility, that is used for demarcating the termination of initial approach. Where no such area is specified the minimum sector altitudes shown on approach charts are applicable.

Intermediate approach is that part of the instrument approach procedure from the first arrival at the first navigational facility, or predetermined fix, to the beginning of the final approach.

Final approach is that part of the landing procedure made in line with the axis of the runway in use when approaching to land.

Holding

An aircraft may be asked to 'Hold' at a navigational facility en route, or at the first facility at the destination aerodrome, to await its turn to commence an approach to land. In either case the rules of holding are the same:

Basic pattern. This is the racetrack pattern.

Max. airspeeds. Various maximum IAS are specified which depend upon whether the aircraft is propeller-driven or jet and also upon the flight level.

Turns. All turns are rate one turns. Most of the holding patterns in the UK are right-hand patterns, that is, right turn after initial entry. But there are a few left-hand patterns as well. Information on this is available from the UK AIP and Area and Approach Charts published by Aerad, Jeppesen, etc.

Timing. Outbound timing shall be 1 min for aircraft up to and including FL 140; $1\frac{1}{2}$ min for aircraft flying above FL 140; and there is no distinction made between propeller-driven aircraft and jet aircraft.

Wind effect. Allowance must be made, both in heading and timing, for wind effect.

Departing the holding pattern. Adjust the pattern within the limits of the established holding procedure in order to leave the holding pattern at the specified time.

Minimum holding altitude. The minimum altitude is not less than 1000 ft above all obstacles.

Onward clearance time. When holding at a terminal facility, EAT is passed to the pilot. This term has already been defined in the last chapter. When holding at an en route facility, 'Onward Clearance Time' will be passed to the pilot by the ground control. This is the time when the aircraft is estimated to leave the facility and continue the route. 'Delay not Determined' message, which may be given at a terminal facility, is not appropriate when the aircraft is held en route, because en route holding mainly occurs to effect separation.

*Diversions

(1) *Definition.* Diversion is the act of flying to an aerodrome other than to the planned destination with the intention of landing there.
(2) *Occasions for a diversion.*
    (1) weather below the operating company's minima;
    (2) obstruction on the runway;
    (3) failure of essential ground aid;
    (4) unacceptable delay.
(3) *Origin of Diversions.* A diversion may be initiated by the pilot himself. Diversions proposed from the ground will generally be originated by the airline company; only in exceptional circumstance will diversions be originated by the ATC. When passing the diversion message to the pilot, ATC will specify its origin, the reasons for the diversion and also pass, if requested, wind and weather data for the new route. If the pilot is unable to comply with the request of diversion, he should give his reasons, and state his intentions.

Aerodrome flight information service

An Aerodrome Flight Information Service operates at certain aerodromes where no approach or aerodrome control service has been established. It operates under a licensed Aerodrome Flight Information Service Officer (AFISO). The service provided at such aerodromes is in the form of 'information' useful for the safe and efficient conduct of flights in the Aerodrome Traffic Zone. From this information pilots decide the appropriate course of action. The AFISO is responsible for:

(1) issuing information to aircraft flying in the Aerodrome Traffic Zone to assist pilots in preventing collisions;
(2) issuing information and instructions (instruction or advice only for the purpose of averting a dangerous situation) to aircraft on the manoeuvring area or between aircraft moving on the apron;

(3) informing aircraft of the state of the aerodrome and its facilities;
(4) alerting safety services;
(5) initiating overdue action.

Aerodromes providing air/ground COM service only
These aerodromes are manned by people without ATS qualifications.

Thus, we have a three tier air traffic system. To distinguish between the three categories, RTF callsigns are given as follows:
ATC service being provided – suffix TOWER, APPROACH, GROUND, DIRECTOR, ZONE or RADAR
Where AFIS is being offered – suffix INFORMATION
No ATC or AFIS offered – suffix RADIO.

General rules

Aerodromes having Air Traffic Control Units
Where an ATC unit is established, an aircraft should not enter the aerodrome traffic zone (except for the purpose of observing signals at that aerodrome with a view to landing there) unless the pilot has the permission of the appropriate air traffic control unit. A pilot flying in the aerodrome traffic zone should listen out on the aerodrome frequency on a continuous basis and the radio must not be switched off after landing until the taxiing is complete. Finally, a pilot is not allowed to taxi, or to take-off or land, anywhere in the zone except with the permission of the air traffic control unit.

Aerodromes not having Air Traffic Control Units
Here, again, an aircraft must not enter the zone, except for the purpose of landing or observing the signals in the signals area with a view to landing there, unless the pilot has permission of the person in charge of the aerodrome. Aircraft flying within such a zone for the purpose of observing the signals are to remain clear of cloud and at least 500 ft above the aerodrome.

On arrival, if other aircraft are in the circuit, join the circuit by conforming with the traffic pattern duly formed. Make all turns to the left unless ground signals indicate otherwise, and take-off and land in the direction shown by the ground signals. If no such signals are displayed, take-off into the wind unless good aviation practice demands otherwise.

Where take-off and landing is not on the runway:

(1) When landing, leave clear on the left any aircraft which has already landed or is in progress of landing ahead.
(2) After landing, turn left, carefully checking that there are no other aircraft or vehicles in the way, and taxi clear of the landing area.
(3) For take-off, leave clear on the left any aircraft which is already taking off or is about to take off.

Arriving at an aerodrome having Approach Control service

An aircraft approaching such an aerodrome under VFR should make initial contact when 15 nm or 5 min flying time from the ATZ boundary, whichever is the greater. If your aircraft does not have the Approach frequency, use the Aerodrome Control frequency. ATC will pass landing information and known traffic to assist pilots to maintain separation from other flights, both VFR and IFR. If radar sequencing of IFR flights is in progress, ATC will provide VFR flights with information to enable them to fit into the landing sequence.

Range of TOWER, AFIS and Air/Ground Communications

Finally, pilots are asked to do their part in minimising interference bearing in mind the high demand for, and utilisation of, frequencies. Communications with aerodromes should be kept to a minimum and restricted as far as possible to heights up to 1000 ft in the immediate vicinity of the aerodrome concerned and in any event, within 10 nm and 3000 ft.

9
Flight in Other Types of Airspace

Flight in control zones and TMAs

General

All CTR and TMAs are notified for the purpose of rule 31 of the Rules of the Air Regulations which is the requirement of position reporting under IFR. Certain CTRs and portions of TMAs are notified for the purpose of the rule 21, which means that the aircraft cannot enter the area under VFR no matter how good the weather.

Controlling Authorities

The designation of the controlling authority of a zone depends on the size and complexity of the zone. At smaller zones, e.g. Belfast CTR, the approach control unit is responsible for the task. In larger zones, a zone controller controls the zone traffic. At the largest zones, ATCC controls zone traffic.

The controlling authority for TMA is normally the ATCC.

Permission to Enter

Where permission is required to enter a zone, such permission should be requested 10 min before entry time, and the request must be made in standard form as follows:

(1) callsign or a/c identification;
(2) type of aircraft;
(3) position, level or altitude and flight conditions;
(4) ETA point of entry;
(5) destination;
(6) aircraft's TAS.

If the CTR or TMA boundary is less than 10 min flying time from the FIR boundary, a pilot should request permission to enter CTR/TMA as soon as possible after he has crossed the FIR boundary.

If the aerodrome of departure is less than 10 min flying time, clearance to enter must be obtained before take-off.

Pilots wishing to enter CTR under VFR when destination weather is below VFR, should contact the zone controller before entering the zone, and give notice of arrival.

Entry into CTR/TMAs notified for the purpose of rule 21 is by prior clearance only, unless the flight is being made in accordance with special local flying or entry/exit lane procedures. Under these procedures certain concessions from compliance with IFR are granted to aerodromes situated in the zones.

Flight on airways

General
All airways are notified for the purpose of rules 21 and 32.

*Terrain clearance on airways
(1) Where the lower limit of a section of the airway is defined as a Flight Level, the absolute minimum altitude for the airway base is at least 1000 ft above any fixed obstacle within 15 nm of the centreline.
(2) Lowest usable level is 500 ft above the base, thus providing a terrain clearance of 1500 ft.
(3) Sections adjacent to CTRs where the lower limit is established at not less than 700 ft agl, ATC clearance will maintain an aircraft at least 500 ft above the base of the airway.

*Flight plan and clearance
(1) A flight plan must be filed and a clearance must be obtained for a flight on airways. (Where the lower level is defined as FL, an absolute minimum altitude of 3001 ft applies.)
(2) Clearance will be in one of the following terms:
　　(a) 'Clearance expires . . . (time).' This means that if the aircraft is not airborne by that time, fresh clearance will be needed.
　　(b) 'Take off not before . . . (time).' This means it is not safe for the aircraft to take off until the specific time stated.
　　(c) 'Unable to clear . . . (level planned).' In this case, an alternative will be offered whenever possible.
　　(d) 'Join Airways at . . . (place and level) not before . . . (time).'

*Airway procedures
(1) Fly magnetic tracks.
(2) ATC will effect separation by one of the following ways:
　　(a) vertically, by giving different levels;
　　(b) longitudinally, by providing time separation, or
　　(c) laterally, by allocating different flight paths.
(3) A pilot has the right to request a different clearance from that issued.
(4) When cleared to leave or join an airway, plan the last leg so that you cross the airway boundary as near 90° as possible.
(5) There can be no VFR clearance. VMC climb or descent may, however, be given when radar is not available, subject to the following conditions:
　　(a) by day only and in VMC;

(b) the pilot agreeing to the procedure, and undertaking responsibility to maintain separation.

In this case all essential information will be passed to the pilot when practicable. VMC on top cruising level clearance will not be given.

*Position reporting

(1) Report position on ATCC frequency at designated reporting points, and at 'On Request' reporting points, if so requested.
(2) Position report message must be in the following standard form:
Identity – Name of RP – Actual time of passing RP – level – ETA next RP.

*Holding

(1) If asked to hold en route, report on arrival at holding point, whether asked to or not. Message: Ident – Name of the holding point – Time – FL.
(2) On leaving, report: Ident – leaving (name of holding point).
(3) When vacating old level for a new level, report: Ident – leaving (old level).

*Joining an airway

(1) File a flight plan either prior to departure or when airborne.
(2) Request permission to join 10 min before ETA (either on ATCC or FIR frequency).
(3) The message is as follows:
    (a) Ident;
    (b) type of aircraft;
    (c) position, heading, level or altitude and flight conditions;
    (d) departure aerodrome;
    (e) ETA point of entry;
    (f) route and point of first intended landing;
    (g) aircraft's TAS;
    (h) desired level on airway.

Crossing an airway

(1) Cross at right angles without permission at the base, where the lower limit is defined as Flight Level.
(2) Otherwise, file a flight plan before departure or while airborne, and request crossing clearance 10 min before ETA. The message is as follows:
    (a) Ident;
    (b) type of aircraft;
    (c) position and heading;
    (d) present flight level/altitude;
    (e) present flight conditions;
    (f) place of crossing;
    (g) crossing level;
    (h) time of crossing.
Report when at the boundary: Ident – Crossing . . . Airway – position – time – level.

(3) Unlesss otherwise requested, stay on FIR frequency.

(4) Gliders may cross any airway in VMC by day (except a Purple airway where Royal Flights take place) without compliance with any IFR rules.

(5) Airway crossings by powered aircraft may be made with ATC permission. Aircraft may cross an airway in VMC by day without compliance with full IFR provided that a clearance is obtained from the appropriate ATCC, and the pilot holds a valid Instrument Rating.

(6) In emergency, cross at an intermediate 500 ft level.

(7) Arrangements can be made with ATCC for other penetrations, e.g. VMC crossings for purpose of photo survey.

Flight levels

Flight levels allocated on airways are based on semi-circular rules and not on quadrantal rules. Broadly speaking, ODD flight levels will be flown on tracks having an easterly element and EVEN on tracks having a westerly element, but always check that your route is not the odd exception to the general practice.

Miscellaneous

(1) In the UK, airways usually extend 5 nm either side of the centreline.

(2) An airway is defined as a control area, or part of a control area, in the form of a corridor and marked by radio navigation aids.

(3) The controlling authorities of airways are the ATCCs. Communication frequencies are given in the Communication Section of the UK AIP.

(4) Airways are identified by a letter, followed by a number. 'Purple' airways are brought temporarily into existence for the duration of any Royal Flights, i.e. carrying one or more of the principal members of the Royal Family. Details are promulgated by NOTAM (R Series).

*Flight on advisory routes

General

(1) The service available to flights on advisory routes is the normal FIR service (see later in this chapter) plus flight separation service.

(2) Advisory routes are not part of the controlled airspace. Being uncontrolled, the procedures are not compulsory, and the service provided is not based on accurate knowledge.

(3) If, however, advisory service is required, IFR flight plans must be filed.

  (a) The lowest level at which advisory service is provided is the published minimum cruising level.

  (b) The service is not available above the maximum published level.

  (c) ATC and RTF procedures are the same as for controlled airspace.

  (d) Levels allotted are quadrantal levels up to FL 240 and semi-circular levels above. In this way it differs from flight on an airway. The exception occurs on portions of the route where aircraft change over between two systems.

Flight plan clearance
(1) When the flight is wholly in controlled or advisory airspace, direct clearance will be given.
(2) When the flight originates outside the controlled or advisory airspace, the entry is by prior permission only. File an airborne flight plan with Airway or FIR controller 10 min before ETA ADR boundary.

Radio and navigation equipment
The requirement for radio communication and navigation equipment is the same as for flight on an airway. This requirement is described in Chapter 7.

Listening watch
A listening watch should be maintained on the appropriate frequencies listed in the COM section of the UK AIP.

Position reports
Position reports should be sent at designated reporting points, and at on request reporting points, if so requested. Particular care should be exercised in position reports, for the separation service depends on it.

Supplementary procedures
(1) You may cancel your IFR flight plan any time you wish, but the report that you are VMC does not in itself constitute cancellation of IFR flight plan.
(2) Although flying on IFR flight plan, it is the pilot's direct responsibility to avoid collision with other aircraft not complying with ADR procedures.
(3) If asked to hold at an en route reporting point, standard procedures are adopted. Send the position report on arrival at the holding point, whether asked to do so or not.
(4) Crossing an ADR under IFR. Request crossing permission in the standard airway form 10 min before crossing time and request traffic information. At the boundary, the following message is sent:
  (a) Ident;
  (b) ADR designation;
  (c) position and time;
  (d) crossing level.
  Remain in contact and report crossing and clear. If unable to communicate, cross without permission at 90° at the appropriate quadrantal. Always cross at a navigational reporting point at 90°, or as close to 90° as possible.

Other traffic
Those not flying on IFR and, therefore, not making position reports, should if possible listen out on the FIR RTF channel. If the pilot wishes to contact the ATCC he should use the appropriate ADR channel.

Radar

(1) Area control radar unit will provide service on certain routes.
(2) Joint Civil/Military Radar units will provide radar service to all co-operating civil and military aircraft operating on the Upper Advisory Routes within the joint radar service area.
(3) Subject to other commitments, Joint Civil/Military Radar units may assist, within their area, aircraft not operating on an upper ADR and not under FIR Radar Control Service or surveillance.

Danger areas

Danger areas and other hazards as applicable to the ADRs are given in the UK AIP, and the official map of the Danger Areas. It is the pilot's responsibility to check if these areas are active, and to keep out of them. Advisory service only relates to separation between traffic complying with the procedures.

Description of ADRs

(1) An advisory route is defined as a designated route along which Air Traffic Advisory Service is available.
(2) An ADR is 10 nm wide, that is, 5 nm either side of the centreline.
(3) Magnetic tracks are flown.
(4) Minimum cruising levels are given in the RAC section of the UK AIP. Those levels marked with an asterisk indicate that they do not provide standard 1500 ft terrain clearance within 15 nm of the track. It is the pilot's responsibility to select the correct cruising level.
(5) Advisory routes are identified by the use of a standard designator, A, B, G, N, or W, followed by a number. D indicates a Lower ATS Advisory Route, e.g. A1D.

Altimeter setting procedures

For flight at and below 3000 ft amsl set regional QNH. Set 1013.2 for flight above 3000 ft.

Controlling authorities

(1) ADRs in London FIR – London ATCC (London Control)
     but some ADRs in London FIR come under Manchester sub-centre (Manchester Control)
(2) ADRs in Scottish FIR – Scottish ATCC (Scottish Control)

Flight in upper airspace

Within the UK UIR, an Upper Airspace Control Area is established extending vertically from FL 245 to FL 660 as Class B Airspace. This area contains a network of Upper ATS Routes between FL 250 and FL 460. The part of the UK UIR not occupied by the Upper Airspace Control Area is designated the Hebrides Upper Control Area (UTA). For a flight in this area, a flight plan must be filed, a continuous listening watch is kept and the flight is conducted in accordance with the ATC instructions, having first entered the area with permission. Where a route has been established, it is 10 nm wide and the designation includes the letter U as the first letter, e.g. UB29 meaning Upper ATS Route Bravo 20. Standard setting is used and semi-circular flight levels are flown except when ATC find it necessary to allocate a level not appropriate to the track.

Military aircraft

Military aircraft are normally under the control of NATS or autonomous Radar Units but outside Military Mandatory Radar Service Areas (MRSAs), they are not obliged to receive an ATC service. NATS radars cover almost all Upper Airspace. Within this cover, there are procedures to co-ordinate civil and known military aircraft and they receive a radar control and/or a procedural ATC service. Outside radar cover, a procedural ATC service is provided.

Outside MRSAs, ATC cannot always offer avoiding action because military aircraft manoeuvres are often unpredictable, but whenever possible ATC will pass information on them to aircraft under control. The concentration of high speed military aircraft operating south of N55° over the North Sea is such that civil aircraft should only flight plan on the ATS routes but when flight conditions permit, ATC may authorise more direct tracks.

Flight in airspace other than CAS, UHMRA and ADRs

This is designated Class G Airspace and is also known as 'open' FIR.

FIR controller

FIR control is established at ATCCs and the air traffic controller on duty is called the FIR controller. He provides Flight Information Service (FIS), alerting service, and some supplementary service, to aircraft in that part of the FIR which is outside the controlled airspace. An FIR controller does not exercise positive control over aircraft and he does not issue clearances nor give positive advice on the avoidance of collision. Having received the information and the benefit of supplementary service the final decision is the pilot's.

Flight information service

This service includes information on the following topics:

(1) meteorological warnings;
(2) meteorological conditions at destination and alternate;
(3) meteorological reports, e.g. VFR possible along the flight path;
(4) airfield serviceability;
(5) airfield facilities;
(6) other information pertinent to the safety of air navigation, such as dangerous proximity to other air traffic, even known traffic in the vicinity.

Supplementary service
In addition to providing FIS and alerting service, the FIR will provide the following additional services:

(1) Obtain clearances to join or cross airways. In this instance, the pilot stays with FIR on RTF unless he is specifically requested to change over to ATCC.
(2) Pass ETAs.
(3) Accept airborne flight plans.
(4) Give warning of proximity hazards. It should be remembered that outside controlled airspace and advisory airspace, aircraft fly on a multiplicity of tracks and altitudes and not all communicate with the ATS.

To contact FIR for Service. A request for service is preceded by the following standard message:

(1) callsign and type of aircraft;
(2) estimated position;
(3) altitude/flight level;
(4) heading;
(5) flight conditions;
(6) point of departure, route and destination;
(7) any other relevant information.

Flight outside controlled airspace
Avoid flying parallel to or near an airway or at its base where the base is defined as a flight level.

Low level civil aircraft notification procedure (CANP)
While for training and operational roles military aircraft may need to operate at very low heights, civil aircraft may also be required to do so on authorised aerial work such as crop spraying, surveys etc. These flights take place in FIRs outside Controlled Airspace where collision avoidance at these low levels is essentially based on 'see and be seen' with pilots avoiding conflicting traffic. The greatest risk of conflict is at or below 500 ft agl and the CANP system has been devised to enable military operators to plan their flights to avoid known civil aircraft. However, civil aircraft carrying out aerial work between 500 and 1000 ft agl where pilot lookout or aircraft manoeuvring capability may be degraded, also potentially conflict with military low flying operations.

London Air Traffic Control Centre (Military) (LATCC (Mil)) co-ordinates information relating to military low-flying and CANP. A Freephone (Freefone 2230) is provided to encourage civil operators to participate.

The CANP message prefixed CIVIL LOW FLYING should comprise:

(1) type of activity;
(2) location (6 fig. OS grid ref. preferred) near . . . (town/village);
(3) area of operation(s) – as radius around location if possible;

(4) date and start/finish time;
(5) operating heights – lower and upper limits agl;
(6) type(s) of aircraft;
(7) contact telephone number;
(8) operating company and its telephone number.

The preferred notification to LATCC(Mil) is not less than 4 hours nor more than 24 hours ahead of the start of the planned low level operation. For operations before 1300 hours (local time), notification should be made on the previous day, while for operations after 1300 hrs pre-notification should be made as early as possible on the morning of the same day. If a notified operation is subsequently cancelled, the maximum possible notice should be given to LATCC(Mil). Also to provide greatest facility to military flying, it is generally expected that agricultural aviation operations can be contained within 2 nm radius circle, while for underslung aerial load lifting operations, as a corridor extending either side of the intended track to a maximum total width of 4 nm from ground level to 1000 ft agl.

10
Use of Radar in Air Traffic Services

In modern aviation, radar is a vital element in safe operations and in general, the United Kingdom subscribes to the ICAO procedures. However an important difference from ICAO applies outside Controlled Airspace where the UK radar service provides either an advisory service or an information service. Table 10.1 sets out the service in the various classes of airspace.

Operation
(1) A Radar Unit operates as an integral part of the ATSU.
(2) The controller will always identify himself at commencement of the service, e.g. (aircraft under area control) 'This is . . . Radar'.
(3) On termination of the service the pilot will be instructed 'Continue with . . . airways' or other relevant instructions.
(4) When service is provided outside the controlled airspace, the radar controller presumes that you will follow the instructions.

Services
(1) In controlled airspace the service provided is called 'Radar control service'.
(2) Elsewhere the service provided is 'Radar Advisory or Information Service'.

Radar control service
This service includes the following:

(1) radar separation to arriving, departing and en route aircraft;
(2) monitoring en route and approach aircraft;
(3) radar vectoring;
(4) assistance in distress;
(5) assistance in crossing controlled airspace;
(6) proximity hazard warning;
(7) information on observed weather;
(8) assistance in navigation.

Radar advisory service (RAS)
This service is provided particularly to aircraft on ADR, in advisory airspace and when flying in the vicinity of aerodromes. Elsewhere the service is provided subject to the workload. The service may be requested under any meteorological

Table 10.1

Airspace class	Type of service	ATC action on unknown aircraft
Class A Airspace, Controlled Airspace subject to IFR at all times and Class D Airspace, Controlled Airspace below FL 245 in which all flights are subject to ATC authority.	Radar Control Service	Traffic information and avoiding action not given unless information received indicating a radar echo may be from an aircraft which is lost or has radio failure.
Class E Airspace, Controlled Airspace in which VFR without ATC clearance is permitted.	Radar Control Service	Traffic information will be passed provided it does not compromise radar traffic sequencing or separation of IFR flights. Avoiding action will be given at pilot's request but to limits set by radar controller or if information received indicating a radar echo may be from an aircraft which is lost or has radio failure.
Class B Airspace, Upper Airspace Control Area.	Radar Control Service	(1) In MRSAs – aircraft operating off promulgated ATS routes will be vectored clear of those operating on the routes. To eliminate possibility of radar-induced conflict, procedure is as Class A Airspace given above. (2) Outside MRSAs – Whenever practicable, traffic information will be given. Avoiding action will also be given if ATC consider necessary or if requested by pilots.
Class F Airspace, Advisory Routes.	Radar Advisory or Radar Information Service	Traffic information passed, followed by advice on avoiding action.
Class G Airspace, All other airspace.		Traffic information passed, but no avoiding action given, with the pilot responsible for his own separation.

conditions or flight rules. However, controllers expect the pilots to accept radar vectors or flight level allocations which may require flight in IMC. *Any pilots who are unable to fly in IMC should only accept an RAS whilst weather conditions allow compliance with ATC advice.* The service is similar to the Control Service.

Information on unknown traffic will be passed to the pilot and advice on avoiding action will be given if the pilot so requests or the controller considers it necessary. The service is merely advisory and the final responsibility for the prevention of collision remains with the pilot.

A Lower Airspace Radar Service (LARS) is available in UK uncontrolled airspace up to FL 95 within 30 nm of each participating unit, at present about 30 aerodromes, during working hours, and occasionally out of working hours. A pilot intending to use the service should note the participating units close to the intended track and follow the procedures:

(1) When 30 nm from the unit, establish two-way RTF communication and 'Request Lower Airspace Radar Service'.
(2) When told 'Go Ahead', give:
    (a) callsign and type of aircraft;
    (b) estimated position;
    (c) heading;
    (d) Flight Level or Altitude;
    (e) intention (i.e. next reporting point, destination etc.);
    (f) request the type of service required i.e. Radar Advisory Service or Radar Information Service.
(3) Maintain listening watch on allocated frequency.
(4) Follow ATCO's advice – or if unable to do so, advise ATC of non-compliance.
(5) Advise ATC when service is no longer required.

Pilots should remember that they must establish verbal agreement with the controller, no radar service being provided until agreement has been reached. No change of heading or FL should be made without prior warning to the controllers. Quadrantal rules of flight must be maintained; a minimum horizontal separation of 3 nm will be sought between identified aircraft working the same unit, or 5 nm horizontal separation between the identified aircraft and other observed aircraft unless 1000 ft vertical separation is known to exist.

Whenever possible, aircraft are handed over from controller to controller, in an area of overlapping radar cover, and the pilot is told to contact the next unit. If this is impossible, the pilot is told his position and advised of the next unit to call for further service.

Radar separation standards

Horizontal separation is 5 nm. This may be increased if the situation warrants. It may be reduced to 3 nm when within 40 nm of the radar head and below FL 245, when authorised by NATS Headquarters. It is increased to 8 nm when SSR only is available.

Radar information service (RIS)

This service may be offered when the provision of RAS is impracticable and a pilot may subsequently request for it to be upgraded to RAS. RIS provides a pilot with information on the bearing, distance (and, if known, the level) of conflicting traffic but no advice on avoiding action.

Terrain clearance

Intermediate Approach and Depart phase
When the aircraft is operating within 30 nm of the radar antenna and within 30 nm of the aerodrome of departure or arrival, the aircraft is in the arrival/ departure phase. The terrain clearance in this area shall be 1000 ft above any fixed obstacle within 5 nm of the aircraft and above any fixed obstacle within 15 nm ahead of and 20° either side of the aircraft's track. Criteria of 5 nm and 15 nm may be reduced to 3 nm and 10 nm respectively with approval. (See Fig. 10.1.)

Whether using the Radar Advisory Service or the Radar Information Service, the responsibility for terrain clearance remains with the pilot.

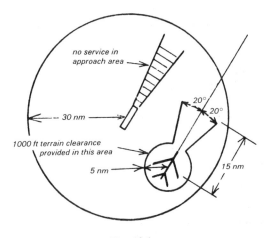

Fig. 10.1

En route phase
On airways and ADRs: 1500 ft above highest obstacle within 15 nm on either side of the centreline. Elsewhere: 1500 ft above highest obstacle within 30 nm of the aircraft.

Operational service area
The area of radar coverage will depend on the type of equipment and weather (rain, clutter). If the radar becomes unserviceable due to clutter on the radar screen, non-radar separation will be established before the service is terminated.

Methods of identification
All aircraft must be positively identified before the service can commence. Identification is achieved by one of the following methods:

(1) pilot's report over a reporting point;
(2) by instructing the aircraft to carry out a manoeuvre;
(3) blip on the radar screen, reflected by the departing aircraft;
(4) Secondary Surveillance Radar identification;
(5) radar handover by one area controller to another;
(6) pilot reporting his position as ascertained by means of the VOR/DME equipment.

Traffic information
Typical information will read something like this: 'Unknown aircraft at 10 o'clock crossing left to right. If not sighted turn left/right . . .'.

Navigation information
When on authorised routes, an aircraft's navigation may be taken over by radar for a variety of reasons, e.g. to provide separation or to expedite the traffic. When radar navigation is terminated, the pilot will be informed 'resume your own navigation' and he will be given information on his present position. Other occasions when a pilot is informed of his position are:

(1) on initial identification;
(2) when requested by the pilot;
(3) when the aircraft is flying off track;
(4) when inaccurate ETAs are passed by the pilot.

Whenever practicable, a radar controller aims to keep aircraft under his control, at least 2 nm within the boundary of Controlled Airspace.

Weather avoidance
(1) The pilot will be informed if the radar shows bad weather ahead.
(2) If within a controlled area, the pilot will be informed should the detour round the weather involve leaving the controlled airspace.
(3) If the aircraft's own weather radar indicates bad weather and the pilot decides to detour round it, he must obtain the controller's permission. If the detour takes him outside the controlled airspace, he will require permission to rejoin.
(4) Navigation assistance in the form of radar flight information service may be provided outside controlled airspace.

Radio failure
If one-way failure occurs, and the pilot can still receive, the radar service will be continued. Otherwise the aircraft will carry out basic radio failure procedures.

Secondary surveillance radar (SSR)
(1) In this system, a ground transmitter, called the interrogator, transmits a

series of coded pulses to which the airborne equipment, called the transponder, replies.

(2) Secondary radar is used to establish and maintain identity of the aircraft and its FL, to assist in the control of aircraft and to supplement radar information, both in UIR and FIR.

(3) Generally, primary radar is used to provide separation and control. SSR alone, may, however, be used to separate transponding aircraft as follows:
  (a) in an emergency;
  (b) when primary radar fails and until non-radar separation is established provided that:
    (i) the position and accurancy of secondary information has been verified, and
    (ii) the pilot has been advised.

(4) The carriage of SSR Transponders over the UK is notified for the ANO and Schedule 5 to the following scale:

  (a) The whole of the UK Airspace at and above FL 100   Mode A – 4096 codes and
  (b) UK Controlled Airspace, notified for Schedule 5, below FL 100 when IFR   Mode C with altitude reporting
  (c) Scottish TMA between 6000 ft ALT and FL 100   Mode A – 4096 codes

The requirement does not apply to gliders or to aircraft below FL 100 in Controlled Airspace, notified for Schedule 5, receiving an approved crossing service.

Operation of transponders

(1) On entering UK Airspace select the specified code, and if the code is not specified, select Mode A, 2000 and Mode C.

(2) Re-select codes, or switch off the SSR when airborne, only when instructed by ATC.

(3) Always acknowledge code setting instructions by reading back the code to be selected.

(4) Select Mode C with Mode A unless otherwise instructed by ATC.

(5) When reporting levels under routine procedures or if requested by ATC, state the current altimeter reading to the nearest 100 ft to enable the ATC unit to verify the Mode C data being transmitted by the aircraft. If on notification there is a difference of more than 200 ft between the level readout and the reported level, the pilot will normally be instructed to switch off Mode C. If independent switching of Mode C is not possible, the pilot will be told to select Code 0000 to indicate a transponder malfunction.

Special Purpose SSR Codes

The following codes have been reserved internationally for special purposes and should be operated with Mode C in each case:

(1) Code 7700 – To indicate an emergency condition. (If the aircraft is already in contact with ATC and has a specific code, that code will normally be retained.)
(2) Code 7600 – To indicate radio failure.
(3) Code 7500 – To indicate unlawful interference with the operation of the flight.
(4) Code 2000 – When entering UK Airspace from where SSR operation has not been required.

Conspicuity Code
When operating at and above FL 100 select Code 7000 and Mode C unless:

(1) ATC or Air Defence Unit requires a different setting.
(2) Circumstances require use of a Special Purpose Code.

Military Middle Airspace Radar Advisory Service
This is a service similar to LARS available from military air traffic control radar units to all aircraft operating between FL 100 and FL 240 (except Brize Radar limited to FL 150) outside regulated airspace in UK FIR (except when on ADRs). Participating aircraft must have a serviceable transponder.

Approach radar
Approach radar operates at selected aerodromes and provides service similar to the radar control service and radar advisory service. In addition, the following specific service may be provided:

(1) vectoring and sequencing of terminal traffic for standard approach aids;
(2) monitoring ILS approaches in certain weather;
(3) surveillance radar approaches;
(4) precision radar approaches.

Operation
As soon as practicable after being accepted for radar, the controller will pass weather information to the pilot. If, during the approach, radar becomes cluttered with weather the pilot will be asked to monitor the approach on another aid, and if no other aid is available, the pilot will be given overshoot instructions.

The pilot will also be given OCL and will be asked to check the company minima. In case of radio failure during an approach, the pilot may continue visually if he can do so; otherwise he should climb to safety height and adopt basic procedures.

The radar controller has authority to give overshoot instructions and such instructions must be obeyed.

Radar Sequencing

Aircraft on final approach will be given headings to close the track at not less than 5 nm. When doing an ILS approach, radar may position the aircraft over the ILS localiser to save time or the pilot may choose to do it himself.

Radar approaches

PAR (Precision Approach Radar)
(1) Precise heading and glide path instructions are given.
(2) Instructions will be terminated at 400 m from the end of the runway except:
   (a) when carrying out emergency precision approach and landing;
   (b) when carrying out practice emergency approach in weather conditions better than 1 nm visibility and 500 ft cloud base;
   (c) when ATC requests a pilot to carry out procedure in (b) for ATC training.

SRA (Surveillance Radar Approach)
With this type of equipment there is no height finding facility and, therefore, glide path information is not given. The information available is the azimuth (left/right of the centreline) and range information. In place of glide path information, check heights are passed. The approach may terminate at $\frac{1}{2}$ mile range or 2 mile range, depending on the type of equipment.

ILS Approach Monitored by PAR
(1) Whenever PAR is available ILS approaches will be monitored on PAR, either when the weather is at prescribed minima or when requested by the pilot.
(2) No instructions will be issued to the pilot as long as he remains within the approach funnel. The approach funnel is approximately $\frac{1}{2}°$ above and below the glide path and 2° either side of the PAR centreline.
(3) The radar controller will advise the pilot that his approach is being monitored. His duty includes warning the pilot if he goes outside the funnel, advising him if a dangerous situation arises and taking over the control if the pilot so requests.

11
Airspace Restrictions, Airmiss Procedures, Low Level Flying Rules

Airspace restrictions

Navigation maps of the UK, if you have noticed, are cluttered with dots, circles, squares and all other imaginable geometrical figures, representing one or other kind of flying restrictions. These are the areas to watch very closely when airborne. All airspace which is potentially hazardous, whether temporarily or permanently, is graded in three classes according to the seriousness of the activities in the area: Danger Areas, Restricted Areas and Prohibited Areas.

Danger Area

A Danger Area is an airspace of defined dimensions within which activities dangerous to the flight of aircraft may exist at notified times.

These are generally the areas where captive balloons fly and weapon ranges operate. The authoritative sources on Danger Areas are two documents: UK AIP (RAC Section) and the 'Chart of Airspace Restrictions in the United Kingdom' issued by the CAA. Amendments to these come in the information circulars.

Pilots should be aware that although the AIP lists the hazardous activities *most likely* to be encountered, other hazards may also be met in that area. Be aware also that small arms ranges etc. which have an upper limit of 500 ft agl or less can constitute a danger and those notified to the CAA are listed in the AIP.

Areas enclosed in solid red outline. These Scheduled Danger Areas are active during the published hours.

Areas enclosed in pecked red outline. These Notified Danger Areas are inactive unless their use is notified by NOTAM.

The RAC section tabulated data and the Airspace Restriction chart also indicate those Danger Areas which have a crossing service available (DACS) and those for which there is an Activity Information Service (DAAIS). It is emphasised that NATSUs giving DAAIS do not have authority to issue crossing clearances. Some Danger Areas also have airspace subject to Byelaws which prohibit entry during the period of Danger Area activity.

Restricted area and prohibited area

A restricted area is an airspace of defined dimensions above the land areas or territorial waters of a State within which the flight of aircraft is restricted in accordance with certain specified conditions.

A prohibited area is an airspace of defined dimensions above the land areas or territorial waters of a State within which the flight of aircraft is prohibited.

Thus, the essential difference between the two is that in the former area a limited penetration is permitted whereas in the latter there is total prohibition. Both types generally stretch from ground level to 2000 ft agl (although in practice they are indicated as above sea level). Of the prohibited areas the following two types should be noted:

(1) Nuclear installations. There is a prohibition of flying below 2000 ft agl and generally within 2 nm radius of these establishments.
(2) Northern Ireland.

These areas are shown in solid purple outline on the Airspace Restrictions Charts. Aircraft can, however, fly within some of the restricted airspace for the purpose of landing or taking off from the helicopter landing area at the installation with the permission of the person in charge and in accordance with any conditions to which that permission is subject.

The UK AIP warns particularly:

'Pilots are urgently warned against inadvertent entry into prohibited or restricted areas in Northern Ireland. Such entry could entail a danger that the flight might be judged to have hostile or criminal intent and the aircraft could be liable to counter-measures.'

Other potentially hazardous areas
These include Military Training Areas (only above FL 245) (in black outline), Bird Sanctuaries (in green outline) and High Intensity Radio Transmission Areas (in blue outline).

Air navigation obstructions
Apart from the above restrictions, there are numerous physical obstructions in the form of tall structures etc. of which the pilot should take a note. Details of these obstructions which reach or exceed 300 ft agl, more than 4 nm from an aerodrome and of which the CAA has been informed, are published in the UK AIP. Within 4 nm any obstruction constitutes a danger. Obstructions which are 150 m (492 ft) or more above ground level are lighted day and night by flashing white (strobe) lights. Those below 150 m (492 ft) are lighted by night, if necessary, by a medium intensity red flashing light. Bridge towers, pylons supporting cables etc. have flashing white lights.

Certain mountains and hills are also marked with red obstruction lights.

Other hazards
Other hazards to a flight are present in the form of a variety of aerial activity such as glider launching where a towing cable may be dropped from a height of 2000 ft and even this height may be exceeded at a few sites; pilotless target aircraft fly up to 60 000 ft; parachute training balloons climb to a height of 1000 ft. There are several areas where intense high speed air activity takes place and yet other areas

devoted to activities such as launching meteorological balloons, hang-gliding, micro-light flying, parascending and launching parachute flares at night. The details of all these and other hazards are to be found in the UK AIP. There are separate charts showing firstly, UK areas of intense aerial activity (AIAA), aerial tactics areas (ATA) and the military low flying system, and secondly, UK winch-launched activities.

Airmiss procedures

On any occasion when you think that you were endangered by the proximity of another aircraft and a definite risk of collision existed, you should file an airmiss report. If a UK public transport aircraft over 2300 kg is involved, you *must* file one under the mandatory occurrence reporting procedure.

If you carry radio, the message in the standard form is sent out on radio to the ATCC, the FIR controller, any air traffic unit or a military air traffic unit. If radio is not carried in the aircraft, or it is otherwise impossible to send out the message while airborne, the report of airmiss must be filed immediately on landing. The standard form of the message is as follows:

(1) AIRMISS
(2) Callsign
(3) Position of airmiss
(4) Aircraft heading
(5) Flight level/altitude
(6) Weather conditions
(7) Time UTC
(8) Description of the other aircraft
(9) Description of the incident.

If the incident occurs while the aircraft is bound for abroad, the pilot may file the report from an overseas station on landing. In this case, he will be permitted the facility of the AFTN.

Having filed the initial report, the pilot or his company should follow it up by completing CA Form 1094 within 7 days of the incident. In the absence of this, the initial report will fail unless exceptional circumstances are shown. But the CA 1094 is a confirmation: it should not be used in place of the initial report since it is not quick enough.

Consequent on the report, the pilot or his company will be kept informed of whatever action is being taken, the pilot may be required to give evidence, and he will be informed of the final outcome.

Reports are to be made if an airmiss occurs abroad. The commander/operator must initiate, confirm and follow through airmiss reports in accordance with national procedures, and the CAA must have a copy of these reports and the responses to them.

Aircraft Proximity Hazard (APHAZ)

Although only pilots can report an airmiss, if in the UK an Air Traffic Control

Officer (ATCO) considers an aircraft may have been endangered by the proximity of another aircraft such that there was a risk of collision, the ATCO should submit a report called an Aircraft Proximity (APHAZ) report to the CAA Safety Data and Analysis Unit. This Unit will then investigate, calling for reports from the pilots, although if the same incident has been the subject of an AIRMISS report, the Airmiss investigation will embody the APHAZ.

Low level flying rules

The rules of low level flying are designed to protect three categories i.e. built-up areas (towns, cities an settlements), assemblies of people and the individual person, vessel, vehicle or structure. The rules are as follows:

Towns, cities and settlements

If you are flying along a route that is notified as such in the AIP, or you are obeying ATC instructions when on special VFR, the lowest height you can fly is that height from where, in case of failure of a power unit, you can clear the area without causing danger to persons or property on the surface. On any other flight, the lowest height is:

(1) either 1500 ft above the highest fixed object within 2000 ft of the aircraft, or
(2) that height from which you could clear the area without causing danger to persons or property on the surface, or if the aircraft is towing a banner such height that the banner shall not be dropped within the congested area;

and of these two alternatives, whichever is the higher.

   (It has been held in court that flying on a special VFR clearance over central London in accordance with (a), did not prevent the flight being illegal under (b).)

   Helicopters. The CAA may give permission in writing to exempt helicopters from (a) above and instead impose other conditions in the written permission.

Assembly of persons

Unless you are a police aircraft, or you are taking part in an air display, you cannot fly over or within 3000 ft of any assembly in the open air of more than 1000 persons, except with the written permission of the CAA and written consent of the organisers, and then not below such height as would enable you to alight clear of the assembly in the event of the failure of a power unit. If your aircraft is towing a banner, the height also must be calculated on the basis that the banner must not be dropped within 3000 ft of the assembly.

   However, if you did happen to fly over or within 3000 ft of such an assembly, it is a recognised defence to show that:

(1) the flight was made at a reasonable height, and that
(2) you were not connected with the assembly in any way.

Persons, vessels, vehicles and structures

If you are not engaged in take-off and landing, or a glider aircraft hill soaring, or picking up or dropping tow ropes, banners, etc. at an aerodrome, or a police aircraft, or taking part in an air display, you must not fly closer than 500 ft to any person, vessel, vehicle or structure.

Exceptions

Exceptions have been mentioned above as they arose with regard to a particular category. Further general exceptions arise which are applicable to all three categories. These are:

(1) Taking off, landing and practising approaches at an appropriate place.
(2) Flying for the purpose of saving life.
(3) Captive balloon or kite.

Also the Rules of the Air Regulations permit an aircraft to fly closer than 500 ft to any person, vessel, vehicle or structure and over, or within 3000 ft of, an assembly of persons gathered for the purposes of witnessing or participating in an event if the flight is made with the consent of the organisers and the event consists:

(1) wholly or partly of an aircraft race or contest, or
(2) wholly or partly of an exhibition of flying for which a permission under Article 56 of the Order is required and the flight is made in accordance with the terms of that permission and in accordance with the conditions of a display authorisation granted to the pilot, or
(3) wholly or principally of an exhibition of flying for which a permission under Article 56 of the Order is not required.

12
Meteorology

Organisation

The meteorological offices throughout the country are organised on the following basis:

(1) *Main offices.* These are located at ATCCs and at major civil aerodromes. They are open at all times and their function includes the supply of forecasts and other met information to their own aerodromes and to the observing offices attached to them. Charts are prepared every three hours, and at intermediate periods if necessary. Further, main offices control and advise subsidiary and observing offices.

(2) *Subsidiary offices.* These are located at all civil aerodromes of intermediate importance. They operate during such hours as meet local requirements. Their functions include the issue of forecasts and other met information similar to the main offices.

(3) *Observing offices.* These are located at minor civil aerodromes. If an observing office is a synoptic reporting station, it operates through 24 hours, otherwise it is open to meet local requirements. It issues weather reports but not forecasts. For forecasts and met information it refers to the main or subsidiary office to which it is attached.

(4) *Meteorological watch office.* The main office at the ATCC is given this designation, and it maintains a continuous watch over the weather within the area assigned to it. Its functions are to:
   (1) advise ATC on diversions;
   (2) liaise with other met offices in the area;
   (3) provide en route forecast service;
   (4) initiate SIGMET messages (see section on In-flight procedures).

Observing routine

At principal aerodromes observations are made on a half-hourly basis, elsewhere on an hourly basis. Special reports are made on sudden deterioration or improvement.

Met procedures

Standard procedures are laid down for all the various stages of flight, from pre-flight through to landing, the aim of the procedures being to provide maximum possible assistance towards safe and economic operation. The procedures are described stage by stage in the following paragraphs.

Pre-flight procedures

In the UK, the basic method of meteorological briefing for pilots is by self-briefing using facilities, information and documentation available or displayed as a matter of routine in aerodrome briefing areas. Briefing for flights below 15 000 ft amsl is also available from the AIRMET recorded telephone service (see later in this chapter).

If this primary method is inadequate or a special forecast is required, the following procedure should be adopted:

(1) Give notice of intended flight at least 4 hours prior to a flight of 500 nm or more; 2 hours notice otherwise.
(2) On receipt of the notice, the met office collects all relevant information and prepares a forecast.

At the pre-arranged time, the crew visits the met office where there is a display of met information for self-briefing purposes. The personal advice of a forecaster can be obtained from a designated forecast office, but this advice will be given on the understanding that full use has already been made of the met documentation available. If the crew cannot attend the briefing personally, a telephone briefing may be arranged.

Forecasts for the destination and alternate aerodromes are included in the documentation. These aerodrome forecasts are prepared by the aerodromes concerned and not the departure aerodrome. Where these forecasts are not received in time, or otherwise are not available, the departure aerodrome met office will produce the forecasts and state their origin.

Meteorological charts – CAMFAX

CAMFAX is a facsimile transmission network for meteorological charts routinely supplying aerodromes with weather charts and spot wind/temperature charts.

*Documentation

The information provided consists of:

(1) *North Atlantic Route*
    (a) significant weather chart;
    (b) isotach charts indicating wind speed and direction at appropriate levels;
    (c) tropopause or max wind chart when appropriate;
    (d) aerodrome forecasts.
(2) *Europe*
    (a) significant weather chart;
    (b) upper winds and temperatures for spot locations;
    (c) 0° isotherm levels in 1000s of feet;

(d) height and temperature of tropopause;

(e) aerodrome forecasts.

A simple forecast is provided for flights under 5000 ft. Height indications on all the above documents are:

(1) En route section – pressure altitudes related to 1013.2 mb setting;

(2) Aerodrome forecasts – height above aerodrome elevation. Additional information between destination aerodrome and the alternate will be provided on request.

All forecasts are valid only for a given period of time.

*Aerodrome forecasts

(1) Aerodrome forecasts included in the document cover the destination aerodrome and alternates.

(2) At stopping points where full briefing and documentation service is not available, the following information will be provided:

(a) most recent aerodrome forecast for the next stop;

(b) upon request, most recent weather relevant to next stage;

(c) new documentation and briefing will be provided if the flight is unexpectedly delayed. This information will be kept up to date until the flight departs.

*In-flight procedures

In-flight procedures operate on a two-way basis; the ground passes met information to the aircraft; the aircraft makes regular observations and passes them back to the ground.

Ground to air supply of information. Met information is supplied to an aircraft in one or more of the following ways:

(1) In accordance with Met Watch Office Procedures. As we noted above, the Met Watch Office initiates SIGMET messages. These are passed on to ATCs for transmission to affected aircraft.

(2) When requested by the pilot, information will be supplied in plain language.

(3) Regular VOLMET broadcasts of weather reports are transmitted in plain language on a continuous basis. ATIS broadcasts are an abridged version of VOLMET and are transmitted on RTF/VOR frequencies at selected aerodromes.

Transmission takes place on VHF channels and the frequencies are noted in the Met Section of the AIP.

(4) An En-Route Forecast Service exists by arrangement between the operator and the met office for the supply of upper winds and temperatures to overflying aircraft.

(5) Upon diversion, met information is supplied by the ATC unit at the pilot's request.

Air to ground supply of information. Aircraft flying in Europe or in countries bordering Europe and the Mediterranean are exempt from making weather reports. Aircraft flying in other areas may be asked to take weather observations and make their reports as follows:

(1) *Routine report.* This is sent out at approximately hourly intervals and is generally combined with routine position reports. The message is sent in AIREP code.

(2) *Special report.* This is sent, in AIREP code, using prefix 'AIREP SPECIAL' whenever:
(a) severe icing or turbulence is experienced, or
(b) conditions affecting the safety of aircraft exist which fall within the definition of SIGMET.

(3) *Additional Report.* These are sent only when specially requested by the ATC. The message is in Airep code and commences with prefix 'AIREP ADD'.

In addition to the above, there is a requirement for reporting any weather condition which is significantly different from that given in the forecast. This requirement only operates within the UK and when flying on relatively short routes.

Post flight procedures
On completion of a flight all Airep forms on which inflight observations are recorded are handed in at the met office.

Met warnings
A met warning is defined as a notification of the occurrence or expected occurrence, not previously notified, of special meteorological conditions which may affect the safety of aircraft. These warnings are given to aircraft, both in flight and on the ground.
Warnings to aircraft in flight. These are of two types:

(1) SIGMET information messages. These are sent out to aircraft in flight when one or more of the following phenomena are occurring or are expected to occur at subsonic cruising levels:
(a) active thunderstorm;
(b) tropical revolving storm;
(c) severe line squall (50 kt);
(d) heavy hail;
(e) severe turbulence;
(f) severe airframe icing;
(g) marked mountain wave;
(h) widespread dust/sand storm.
Similarly at transonic or supersonic levels, warning messages are sent in respect of the following phenomena:
(a) moderate or severe turbulence;

(b) cumulus cloud;

(c) hail.

(2) Fog Warning. This is given when visibility is expected to fall below 1000 m. It generally applies to aircraft flying in the vicinity of an aerodrome.

Warning to aircraft on ground. Warning for the protection of parked aircraft is given when gales (35 kt), squalls, snow, gusts (43 kt), etc, are imminent.

Low level aviation meteorological service in the UK

A service providing low level aviation meteorological forecasts and an aerodrome weather information service is available for the UK by telephone (called AIRMET), Aeronautical Fixed Telecommunication Network (AFTN) and Telex. The introduction of the service in June 1987 led to the withdrawal of the telephone meteorological service to aviation previously available from RAF stations and government aerodromes. Special (route) forecasts are not provided within the coverage of the UK low level service.

The low level service which is an alternative to that provided at the Flight Briefing Units gives 10 area forecasts (including three regional forecasts) and 104 aerodrome weather messages (TAFs and METARs) for the UK and near continent. The regions are:

(1) Southern England (south of a line approximately from South Wales to the Wash);

(2) Northern England, Wales and Northern Ireland;

(3) Scotland.

For regional forecasts, the information provided (for an 8-hour period of validity) comprises forecast conditions up to 15 000 feet (except *) of:

(1) meteorological situation;

(2) weather;

(3) warnings;

(4) outlook;

(5) surface visibility;

(6) cloud;

(7) freezing level;

(8) airframe icing;

*(9) winds: 1000 ft

2000 ft

5000 ft

10 000 ft

18 000 ft.

The format is so arranged that a telephone caller (receiving the information at dictation speed) can quickly determine if the forecast weather conditions are unsuitable for the intended flight and if so, ring off.

Area forecasts, of which the format may be revised from time to time (and so published in AICs), comprise five sections:

(1) heading (i.e. area, period of validity etc.);
(2) meteorological situation;
(3) winds: Strong surface wind warnings (threshold 20 kt);
        Spot winds and temperatures, usually for 1000, 3000, 6000 ft amsl;
        Freezing level(s);
(4) weather (visibility, weather and cloud – in this element visibility in cloud covering hills will not be given and is assumed to be 200 m or less); weather warning(s) if applicable;
(5) outlook (especially to around VMC/IMC limits).

An expansion of the automated AIRMET service is available to those whose telephones have tone dialling keyboards and on digital exchanges, through the Telephone Menu Service.

The forecasts are issued at every six hours after updating on a routine basis, but can be revised if the need arises between the standard times. The actual process of recording the UK Regional Forecasts for telephone callers has been allowed an hour, so the AFTN and Telex service distributes the data one hour before the forecast's period of validity.

The meteorological offices providing a service to general aviation also operate an 'on-request' telephone service providing available TAFs and METARs for aerodromes in the forecast regions to pilots not having access to teleprinter aerodrome information.

CAA will also, subject to prior request (at least 2 hours earlier), make arrangements for the supply of specialised meteorological information on:

(1) thermal activity and sea breezes for gliding, balloon, microlight and hang-gliding operations;
(2) 1000 ft wind forecast for offshore operations off eastern England;
(3) particular needs for special events for which the routine broadcasts may be inadequate.

Demand for such information has led to two types of specialised forecast being routinely available:

(1) helicopter operations in the Southern North Sea, obtainable by Telex;
(2) sporting aviation sites/areas, for which information is provided on:
    (a) surface wind;
    (b) thermal activity – depth of convection, thermal strengths, time to reach trigger temperature, inversion level;
    (c) details of sea breezes – existence, timing and extent of anticipated movement inland;
    (d) lee waves – existence, height, geographical extent, estimate of maximum vertical speed;
    (e) forecast lowest QNH for area and period of forecast.

Regular broadcasts of met information

Regular broadcasts of weather reports and tendency are made by London and Preston ATCC on a continuous basis on VHF frequencies. These are known as VOLMET broadcasts, and cover weather for selected aerodromes. Each cycle is preceded by a Time announcement. This is the time at the end of the observing period. Individual aerodrome reports are broadcast for 30 minutes after the observation, and for a period of a further 30 minutes if no fresh observation has come through during that period. If at the end of one hour no fresh report has been received, then the broadcast in respect of that aerodrome is suspended. The contents of the broadcast are: surface wind, visibility, RVR if applicable, weather, cloud, temperature, dew point, and QNH *in that order*.

TREND forecasts are issued where the forecaster is on current duty.

When the following observations are made simultaneously, the term CAVOK is broadcast:

(1) visibility of 10 km or more;
(2) no cloud below 5000 ft or below the highest minimum sector altitude, whichever is higher, and no cunimb cloud;
(3) weather – no precipitation or thunderstorms, shallow fog or low drifting snow.

TREND, when included, indicates the trend of the weather during the next two hours. The message follows the main body of the broadcast, with one of the following indicators:

(1) TREND – trend forecast;
(2) GRADU – gradual change at constant rate;
(3) RAPID – rapid change (in $\frac{1}{2}$ hr or less);
(4) INTER – intermittent change, conditions fluctuating;
(5) TEMPO – change expected to last less than one hour;
(6) NOSIG – no significant change expected;
(7) PROB – percentage probability.

There is no system of forecasting TREND for RVR, which is never *forecast* anyway.

Meteorological codes in current use

The AIREP code has been mentioned above. It is used for the transmission of weather observations by aircraft to the ground. The following three codes are used by the ground organisation for transmission of weather information to other ground stations and to aircraft in flight where appropriate:

(1) METAR – this name was derived from 'MET Aerodrome Report' and is a routine weather report for aviation purposes;
(2) SPECI – this is an aviation selected special report and is used for reporting sudden changes;
(3) TAF – this is the Terminal Aerodrome Forecast.

All these three codes, in practice, are only semi-codes and with a little practice can be deciphered by any pilot. They are explained in detail in the companion volume *Ground Studies for Pilots: Volume 4 – Meteorology.*

Pressure units

Pilots should be aware that as from 1 January 1986, ICAO adopted the *hectopascal* as the approved unit for measuring and reporting pressure. The hectopascal is identical to the millibar (1013 hectopascals equals 1013 millibars) and the term may well be encountered outside the UK. However the UK has told ICAO that for the foreseeable future the UK will continue to use the millibar as its pressure unit.

13
Communications*

The telecommunication service provided in the UK is based on four broad divisions:

(1) *Aeronautical Mobile Service.* This service covers air/ground communication, rescue frequencies and communication between aircraft in flight.
(2) *Aeronautical Radio Navigation Service.* This service provides radio and radar navigation aids which include en route, terminal approach and let-down aids.
(3) *Aeronautical Fixed Service.* This service covers communication between ground stations and utilises radio, telephone, teleprinter and so forth.
(4) *The Aeronautical Broadcast Service.* This is the met broadcast service mentioned in the previous chapter.

In our present syllabus we are only interested in the first two services.

Aeronautical Mobile Service
(1) *RTF communications.* In general, the language you use on the RTF is the language of the country. It will be found that English is spoken in most countries, and in case of difficulty, the operator may appoint an interpreter at the ground station, at his expense.
(2) *Time announcements on RTF.* If, while chatting away with some station on RTF, you hear time signals in the background, this means that your conversation is being tape recorded, the time being printed on the tape. These time signals are not, therefore, primarily for the pilot's benefit.
(3) *Congestion of radio channels.* RTF transmissions should be limited to those essential for the safe conduct of flight. The following factors are contributory to congestion and should be avoided:
   (a) request for met information which could be obtained on normal broadcast;
   (b) non-compliance with standard reporting procedures;
   (c) failure to stop transmitting when requested to do so;
   (d) failure to listen out prior to commencing transmission;
   (e) use of unauthorised abbreviations or incorrect procedure;
   (f) lack of general radio discipline.
(4) *Care in operation.* A particular misuse reported is the leaving of transmitters in the 'Transmit' position. Particular instances where this has occurred are:

(a) hand or headset stored so that the transmitter switch is permanently on;
(b) object(s) put on desk-type transmitter switch;
(c) hand portables discarded with the transmitter switch still on.

Also when instructed to change frequency, do not do so until you have read back to the ATCO the frequency to which you are changing. If this is not done, the ATCO does not know whether you have had a radio failure or have changed frequency and to be on the safe side has to telephone the next authority to find out.

(5) *Use of Aeronautical Emergency Channel 121.5 MHz*
   (a) it provides a clear channel for aircraft in distress;
   (b) it provides a communication channel in emergency between aircraft and ground;
   (c) it provides a communication channel between search aircraft;
   (d) it provides a means of communication when other channels fail;
   (e) it provides a means of communication with ocean weather vessel stations when no other channel is available.

(6) *Interference on Aerodrome VHF Channels.* In order to avoid interference with neighbouring stations operating on the same or adjacent frequencies, pilots should observe the following limits unless in emergency or instructed otherwise:

Tower	Range 10 nm*	Altitude 3000 ft*
Approach	Range 25 nm	Altitude 10 000 ft

* For en route sectors and for international aerodrome services, the limits for Tower are 25 nm and 4000 ft.

Aeronautical Radio Navigation Service

The following are the radio navigation services available in the UK. We will only discuss those applicable to our syllabus.

VOR	NDB
Approach Radar	Precision Approach Radar (PAR) ILS
DME	VHF Direction Finding (VDF)
MLS	

VOR

(1) It enables the aircraft to measure its angular deviation from the station's magnetic north direction.
(2) A VOR is not considered accurate beyond a range of 200 nm. It may be inaccurate at closer ranges due to bending and scalloping of the signals. Where this effect has been noticed, the information is published in the Com Section of the AIP.
(3) In the UK all VORs are monitored to an accuracy of 1°. If the accuracy falls below the limit, the defaulting VOR is swtiched off automatically and a standby transmitter brought in.

(4) In such a case, the standby transmitter takes a little time before the signals are stabilised to give correct directions. During this period the station will not broadcast its identification. When making an approach on VOR it is a requirement that the pilot monitors the station identification signals.

(5) Protection from harmful interference is provided in altitude as well as range. These protection altitudes and ranges are given in the Air Pilot.

NDBs

(1) These beacons are used in conjunction with the ADF equipment in the aircraft as en route and approach aids to airfield facilities.

(2) Protection from harmful interference from other NDBs, broadcasters etc, is provided in range. A minimum protection ratio of three (equal to 10 decibels) is established between the field strength of the wanted and unwanted signals by geographical separation and/or power adjustment of various facilities. This limits the bearing errors to ±5°.

The propagation of medium frequencies is subject to diurnal and seasonal changes and therefore the published protection ranges are valid during daytime only. It is important for this reason that at night the ADF is correctly tuned.

ILS

(1) This is a standard, non-visual (i.e. purely instrumental) aid to final approach and landing. All systems are categorised according to performance capability and the categories are as follows:

   (a) Category I – This is an ILS which provides guidance information from the coverage limit to the point at which the localiser course line intersects the glide path at a height of 200 ft above the horizontal plane marking the ILS reference point.

   (b) Category II – This is defined as above, providing guidance information up to 50 ft.

   (c) Category III – this is an ILS which, with the aid of ancillary equipment where necessary, provides guidance information from the coverage limit to, and along, the surface of the runway.

(2) When making an ILS approach, pilots should regard a half of the full scale 'fly up' indication as representing the maximum safe deviation below the centreline of the glide path.

(3) Pilots wishing to use the ILS localiser as a navigational aid should note that the localisers are only protected from interference out to a range of 25 nm at an altitude of 6250 ft along the on-course line, and they are checked for accuracy only up to 10 nm.

MLS

(1) MLS differs from ILS in that it allows approaches to be made anywhere in the horizontally and vertically fan-shaped coverage area;

(2) usually the range is 200 nm and the approach zone ± 40° of the extended runway centreline;

(3) the approach angle varies from 0.9° to 20°.

TACAN/DME

(1) The DME facility available from this installation may be used in conjunction with VOR to give range and bearing information simultaneously.

(2) Because of military requirements for siting, the DME element of TACAN is not always associated with the VOR with which it is frequency paired.

(3) To enable the pilot to establish the relationship between the two, the arrangement in Table 13.1 exists.

Table 13.1

VOR and DME associated.	Always frequency paired.	The same identifier is transmitted synchronously by both facilities.
VOR and DME at different locations.	May, or may not be frequency paired.	Different identifiers are used.
VOR and DME not associated but serving the same location and which may be used in conjunction with each other.	Frequencies are paired.	First two letters of the ident are the same. One facility uses letter Z as the last letter of the identifier.

The word 'associated' in Table 13.1 means that the VOR and DME are either co-located or situated as closely as possible, maximum separation being:

(1) 30 m where used in terminal areas;

(2) 600 m elsewhere.

Ground DF

This is a ground radio station which provides navigational aid to an aircraft on VHF. A pilot may request QTE, QUJ, QDR or QDM. All bearings given by the ground station are classified as follows:

(1) Class A – accurate within ± 2°;

(2) Class B – accurate within ± 5°;

(3) Class C – accurate within ± 10°.

Purpose and Use. An automatic VHF/DF facility is provided at a number of locations in the UK where its prime purpose is to assist in radar identification. As no other service is provided by these installations, they are not promulgated in the UK AIP.

When, however, an automatic VHF/DF provides a 'homer' service, details are given and the class of bearings is not normally better than Class B. Bearings from automatic VHF/DF are not to be used for en route navigation except in emergency.

Miscellaneous

(1) Certain frequencies may be utilised on a world-wide basis. These are:

   500 kHz – International Distress/Calling frequency;
 2182 kHz – International Distress/Calling frequency;
121.5 MHz – Survival Craft frequency;
  243 MHz – Survival Craft frequency;
121.5 MHz – Aeronautical Emergency frequency.

(2) Portable radio telephones
Mobile telephone services are now widely used in cars, road transport etc. operating with relatively powerful transmitters, through a cellular network. Such ground-based facilities must not be used in aircraft. Not only would the use contravene the aircraft's and the user's licence conditions, not to mention the Air Navigation Order, but also it could disrupt the ground cellular system, disconnect other users and interfere with the aircraft's own systems.

14
Search and Rescue

Two annexes of the Convention are involved in these procedures. Annex 11 – Air Traffic Services – covers Air Traffic Control service, Flight Information Service and Alerting service, while Annex 12 deals more specifically with Search and Rescue. Contracting states each have similar arrangements enabling ready international co-operation when the need arises.

Responsibility for search and rescue in the UK and surrounding waters rests with the joint civil/Service organisation. The country is divided into two search and rescue regions, each having a central headquarters, called the Rescue Co-ordination Centre (RCC). The two RCCs are located at Edinburgh and Plymouth. These are authorised to call out various public bodies for S & R duties. The RAF provides the primary airborne force for these duties. Other elements are the RAF Mountain Rescue Units, RNLI, Coastguards, Police and ocean weather ships. RN helicopters and ships together with civilian aircraft, merchant ships and military personnel make up the secondary force.

*Frequency allocation
Search and Rescue aircraft operate on 121.5 MHz, 243 MHz and 500 kHz. In the search area civil aircraft use 123.1 MHz, military aircraft 282.8 MHz. There are other frequencies in the HF band.

Degrees of emergency
When an incident happens, various organisations are alerted, the nature and state of alertness being determined by the degree of the emergency. Various phases are given below.

International code words used for the varying degrees are:

(1) INCERFA – uncertainty phase;
(2) ACERFA – alert phase;
(3) DETRESFA – distress phase.

The form of the standard international message is in the sequence:

(1) INCERFA/ALERFA/DETRESFA;
(2) agency/person calling;
(3) nature of emergency;
(4) significant information from the flight plan;

(5) unit last contacted with time and frequency used;
(6) last position report and how determined;
(7) colour and distinctive marks of the aircraft;
(8) any action taken by the person reporting;
(9) other pertinent remarks.

(1) Uncertainty phase

Uncertainty phase is raised in one or more of the following circumstances:

(a) when no communication is received from an aircraft within 30 minutes after the time that communication should have been received;
(b) failure to establish communication, when the aircraft should answer;
(c) failure to arrive within 30 minutes of ETA last notified or estimated by the ATS, whichever is later.

During this phase the RCC informs appropriate rescue units and collects and evaluates information.

(2) Alert phase

Alert phase is raised:

(a) when subsequent attempts fail to establish communication;
(b) no news of the aircraft;
(c) received information indicates that the aircraft's operating efficiency has been impaired, or
(d) an aircraft cleared to land fails to do so within 5 minutes, and there is no obvious reason for it.

(3) Distress phase

This is raised in any one of the following circumstances:

(a) further attempts to establish contact are unsuccessful;
(b) fuel is considered to be exhausted;
(c) received information indicates that the aircraft might be forced to land.

The pilot, for his part, should do all that is possible to help the search and rescue organisation in their attempts to find him. While airborne, time permitting, the pilot should pass normal urgency and distress messages giving as much information as possible. Initially, send out the message on the frequency already selected. If none is selected, try to call the nearest airfield. Failing that, use 121.5 or 243 MHz. All ATCCs and certain MoD stations continuously listen out on 121.5. Provided that you have sufficient emergency, you may request an RAF escort aircraft. This service is free of charge but subject to RAF operational requirements. When the service is provided, the escort aircraft will fly close and below the crippled aircraft.

An emergency may be expressed in three degrees: distress, difficulty and urgency. Their meanings, laid down in the Rules of the Air Regulations, together with the appropriate signals are given below.

Distress
This is a condition when an aircraft is threatened by grave and imminent danger and immediate assistance is required. Appropriate signals are:

(1) by RTF the spoken word 'MAYDAY';
(2) by visual signalling:
    (a) the signal SOS (. . . — — — . . .);
    (b) a succession of pyro lights fired at short intervals, each showing a single red light;
    (c) a parachute flare showing a red light;
(3) by sound signalling (other than RTF):
    (a) the signal SOS;
    (b) a continuous sounding with any sound apparatus.

Difficulty
This means that the commander of the aircraft wishes to give notice of difficulties which compel it to land but that he does not require immediate assistance. The signals are:

(1) a succession of white pyro lights;
(2) the repeated switching on and off of the landing lights;
(3) the repeated switching on and off of navigation lights, at irregular intervals.

Difficulty is a UK (non-ICAO) category.

Urgency
This means that the commander of the aircraft has an urgent message to transmit concerning the safety of a ship, aircraft, vehicle or other property, or of a person on board or within sight of the aircraft. The signals are:

(1) by RTF the spoken word 'PAN PAN'
(2) by visual signalling XXX (— . . — — . . — — . . —)
(3) by sound signalling (other than RTF) the signal XXX.

This last case, although a part of the Rules of the Air Regulations, is a UK rule not universally adopted by ICAO.

    After a ditching or crash landing is completed the crew should make the maximum use of some of the equipment on board the aircraft to draw the attention of the search aircraft. Survivors in a life-raft may use one or more of the following:

(1) distress flares and cartridges;

(2) heliograph or similar flat bright surface;
(3) dinghy radio;
(4) fluorescent dye marker;
(5) fly a flag with a ball above or below it – this is an international distress signal.

Survivors of a crash landing in isolated areas should use the following to attract attention when search aircraft or surface craft are seen or heard:

(1) distress flares and cartridges;
(2) heliograph;
(3) dinghy radio;
(4) ground-air signals;
(5) flashing light;
(6) triangular fire or smoke.

*Use of radio

If you have VHF or UHF radio aid on a dinghy, remember that its life is short and therefore must be used sparingly. Recommended use is approximately 4 min every 10 min, and only when search aircraft are expected to be within the range.

The dinghy radio operates on 500 kHz and generates its own power when the handle is cranked. Therefore, as far as the power conservation is concerned, the only limitation is the strength in your arms. However, the recommended times for transmission are the hour plus 15 min, and the hour plus 45 min, for a period of three min. These are the times when by international practice all ships and aircraft listen out on this frequency. If HF radio operating on 2182 kHz is carried, the appropriate times are on the hour, and hour plus 30 minutes, again transmitted for three minutes. Satellites are already proving their worth in accurately locating survivors' signals on Emergency Location Transmitters (ELT) or Emergency Position Indicating Radio Beacons (EPIRB) through the Cosmos Rescue System (COSPAS) and the Search and Rescue Satellite Aided Tracking System (SARSAT) in which the UK is sharing international operations.

The ground-air signals mentioned above are internationally recognised. They are now five only in number, and aligned with the International Code of Signals used by mariners.

$\vee$ Require assistance

$\times$ Require medical assistance

N No or negative

Y Yes or affirmative

$\uparrow$ Proceeding in this direction

The symbols should be 2.5 m (8 ft) long, conspicuous, made by any means – fabric, stones, trampling, staining with oil, and attention drawn by other means – flares, smoke, etc.

A search aircraft understanding the signals will rock its wings by day, or flash its lights on and off twice by night. An aircraft observing you in distress will take the following actions:

(1) Keep you in sight;
(2) Fix the position;
(3) Report to ATCC;
(4) Act on ATCC instructions;
(5) Take charge over arriving aircraft.

Action taken by an aircraft on intercepting a distress call is as follows:

(1) stop transmission on that frequency;
(2) plot given position;
(3) take a bearing on other's transmission if possible;
(4) should no one answer him, act as a relay;
(5) proceed to the aircraft if possible;
(6) if necessary, send out a QRT or 'Stop Transmitting Mayday' signal to clear out other aircraft using the same channel;
(7) act on ATCC instructions.

Having sighted a ditched aircraft, a nearby surface vessel may be guided to the scene of ditching by adopting the following procedures:

(1) circle the vessel at least once;
(2) fly across the bow, opening and closing the throttle, or changing propeller pitch;
(3) head away in the direction you wish the craft to follow.

The vessel will acknowledge your message in one of the following ways:

(1) hoist a vertical red and white striped code pennant, or
(2) flash TTT on signals lamp, or
(3) simply alter heading to follow you.

Any one of the above three signals indicates that the vessel has understood the message and it is taking action to comply. If it is unable to comply, the appropriate signal is the international flag N (which is a blue and white chequered flag) or the letter N flashed on the signal lamp.

Having alerted the vessel, if, subsequently, its assistance is not necessary, convey this to the vessel by crossing its wake at a low altitude, opening and closing the throttle or changing propeller pitch.

RAF aircraft searching at night adopt a special technique and the actions on the part of the search and the distressed aircraft are:

(1) search aircraft fires green pyros at approximately 5–10 min intervals;
(2) on seeing one of these, the distressed aircraft allows 15 seconds for the glare to die down, then fires two red pyros at short intervals;
(3) subsequently, it fires a red only if the homing aircraft is found to be deviating;
(4) finally, a red is fired when the search aircraft is overhead.

Flights in areas in which search and rescue operations are in progress

To avoid interference with SAR operations and to avoid an unnecessary collision hazard, CAA strongly advise pilots not to fly near an area where SAR operations are known to be in progress. Crews of aircraft involved in the SAR operation may be performing complex manoeuvres, often in poor weather conditions, and may not be able to maintain a good look-out for other aircraft.

If it is necessary to fly in a known area of SAR operations, pilots should:

(1) file a flight plan giving the times of entering and leaving the area together with the height to be flown, ensuring that the appropriate RCC is included among the addressees;
(2) obtain from the met office the latest information about weather conditions en route and within the search area;
(3) monitor the VHF International Distress (121.50 MHz) and the Scene of Search (123.10 MHz) frequencies when in the vicinity, but avoid transmitting on these frequencies.

A temporary danger zone may be established around the scene of an incident under exceptional circumstances, by issuing a Class I NOTAM. If this measure does not achieve its objective. Restriction of Flying (Emergency) Regulations may be invoked (promulgated too by Class I NOTAM) making it an offence for an aircraft to be flown in the designated area.

UK Military Emergency Diversion Aerodromes (MEDA)

These maintain a continuous watch on 121.50 MHz and may be alerted by ATCC to provide assistance to an aircraft in difficulty or distress. In a comprehensive pink AIC the CAA sets out procedures which pilots can use for practice or for real. Although not an ICAO requirement, it is urged that inexperienced civil pilots, especially students, should prefix their callsign with TYRO when in distress or in difficulty in contact with a military unit or ATCC. Controllers will then ensure that they do not issue instructions which the pilot may have difficulty in carrying out.

15
Facilitation

This chapter deals with the rules and regulations regarding Customs immigration, airport formalities and documentation and health requirements. These are basically laid down in Annex 9 and are elaborated in the AIP. Students studying Aviation Law for a Private Pilot's licence need only study the portion of the chapter dealing with non-scheduled non-commercial flights, health and security regulations and availability of aerodromes for Customs purposes.

General

Arrival
Unless specially cleared, you should arrive for your initial landing from abroad at a Customs aerodrome only. You may cross the UK coast anywhere, subject to other limitations, e.g. controlled airspace or danger area.

Aircraft – liability for duty
(1) UK based aircraft returning after temporary export are exempt from payment of import duty, provided that no repairs have been carried out while abroad other than normal routine servicing.
(2) Non-UK based aircraft engaged on scheduled international service are exempt from payment of duty.
(3) On temporary importation by persons/companies resident abroad, no duty is payable, provided the following conditions are fulfilled:
    (a) the aircraft is not sold, lent or otherwise disposed of while in the UK;
    (b) the aircraft is not used for demonstration while in the UK;
    (c) the aircraft is not used for remuneration within the UK.
This concession does not apply to imports for aerial work, repair or overhaul.

Departure
(1) The last take-off before leaving UK must be made from a Customs airport unless special permission has been obtained to take-off from a non-Customs airport.
(2) Once an aircraft is finally cleared at a Customs aerodrome, it cannot land at any place in the UK other than the Customs airport named in the General Declaration.

(3) Before leaving on a non-scheduled commercial or private flight:
  (a) present the Department of Transport (DoTp) Licence for export to the Customs, or
  (b) if leaving temporarily, produce a Carnet de Passages en Douane, or Customs Form C 42 in duplicate, on which the pilot undertakes to return the aircraft to the UK within one month;
  (c) the Carnet or the duplicate of Form C 42 should be retained and presented to the Customs on return.

Flight to/from Channel Islands, Isle of Man, or Northern Ireland

For the purposes of Customs, the Channel Islands are considered to be foreign territory. As far as the Isle of Man and Northern Ireland are concerned, an aircraft must land at a Customs airport if it is carrying goods on which insular duties are different from those on the mainland.

Forced landings

If an aircraft is obliged to make a forced landing after having been finally cleared from a Customs airport outbound, or before it could reach a Customs airport when inbound, the following procedure is adopted:

(1) report the landing immediately to Customs or the police;
(2) produce the flight documents to authorised officials if they so request;
(3) do not leave the immediate vicinity of the aircraft without consent of the above authority except for reasons of health, safety or preservation of life;
(4) comply with any directions given.

Prevention of terrorism

An order is in force entitled Prevention of Terrorism (Supplementary Temporary Provisions) (Northern Ireland) Order. All aircraft, private and commercial, with or without passengers, coming to Great Britain from the Republic of Ireland, Northern Ireland, Isle of Man or the Channel Islands or going from Great Britain to any of these places, must on exit from or entry to Great Britain land at an airport designated in that Order.

The object of the order is to enable the police to make security checks on people entering/leaving Great Britain and Northern Ireland. Aircraft captains must obtain clearance from the examining police officer and ensure that the captain, crew and passengers comply with the requirements of the examining officer.

If it is wished to fly from an airport not designated in the Order, prior permission must be obtained from the Chief Constable of the Area in which the airport is located. The list of designated airports and addresses of Chief Constables is given in the AIP.

Aerodrome operating minima

All operators of UK-registered public transport aircraft are required to include in the aircraft's operations manual particulars of operating minima for every aerodrome of 'intended departure or landing' and every alternate aerodrome. Operators must give the aircraft commander written details (and retain a copy for 3 months) of similar operating minima for aerodromes not listed in the operations manual before flight to such aerodromes. The operations manual also has to include data and instructions to enable the commander to calculate operating minima for aerodromes the use of which the operator could not have foreseen before the flight. Factors taken into account in determining minima include:

(1) the aircraft's performance, handling and C of A conditions;
(2) crew configuration;
(3) aerodrome's characteristics and surroundings;
(4) runway dimensions;
(5) aerodrome aids for approach/landing/take off.

For operators of non-UK registered public transport aircraft, the CAA requires specific details to be provided on aerodrome operating minima in respect of take-off, circling and landing for each approach aid and the runway in use for it. Such aircraft may not fly in or over the UK unless such minima are supplied.

Details of operations in accordance with aerodrome operating minima are given in Chapter 16, Articles 31 and 32.

Flights to/from UK

Scheduled flights – arrivals
Documents. Deliver the following documents on arrival from abroad:

(1) a General Declaration if required by Customs;
(2) two copies of the cargo manifest if cargo or unaccompanied baggage is carried;
(3) two copies of Store Lists Form if the aircraft has stores on board;
(4) a written personal declaration on Form C909 by aircrew at certain airports.

Scheduled flights – departure
(1) Give notice of intended departure before any passengers, goods or stores are loaded for any flight to outside the UK. The following documents are required:
  (a) Two copies of cargo manifest if cargo or unaccompanied baggage is loaded.
  (b) Two copies of Stores Lists Form for stores which remain on board or if fresh stores are loaded.
(2) If an aircraft, once cleared by the Customs, lands at another Customs aerodrome which is endorsed on the General Declaration, the Customs officer at the second aerodrome countersigns the form. If no goods or stores are taken there, then no further documentation is required.

*Scheduled flights – transit
Documentation in case of an aircraft in transit is as follows:

(1) a General Declaration on arrival;
(2) on departure two copies are required of the Cargo Manifest;
(3) if goods are loaded or unloaded, full arrival and departure documentation is required.

*Non-scheduled commercial flights
(1) Operators should check on any local limitations or restrictions on operation of such flights at the aerodrome concerned.
(2) Documents on arrival and departure are the same as scheduled flights. In addition to these, the export licensing requirements as discussed at the beginning of the chapter apply to these flights.
(3) Certificate of Competency. The Department of Transport requires evidence that the operating company is considered by the national authority of the State of Registry of the aircraft to be operationally competent to undertake the type of flight concerned.

Technical stops. Those party to the Chicago Convention require no permission to overfly or make a technical stop for non-traffic purposes. Other countries may do so by prior permission only.

Non-scheduled flights: non commercial
Airport requirements are:

(1) The pilot should check on local restrictions or limitations at aerodromes concerned.
(2) Documents required are as per scheduled flight. A General Declaration is required (for Customs) but if no fare paying passengers or goods are carried, even this requirement is dispensed with. Only the Carnet or import vouchers are then necessary.

Technical stops. The rules are the same as non-scheduled commercial flights.

Passengers
An alien is required to produce a landing card, embarkation card, a valid passport and, with certain exceptions, a visa. Further, an alien or a Commonwealth citizen arriving in the UK to enter employment must have a Department of Employment permit.

A passport is not required in respect of certain European countries provided the person holds a national identity card together with a Visitor's Card issued by travel agencies or airlines.

A passenger in transit is not required to produce documents.

*Crew

A flight crew member staying on the airport or in city vicinity, or flight crew of international air transport waiting for the next flight out is not required to produce any documents other than:

(1) his licence with a certificate that he may re-enter his State, or
(2) his Crew Member Certificate with similar endorsement, if he is an unlicensed crew member.

A private pilot should note that a PPL is not acceptable for establishing identity, and private pilots must carry passports and visas.

*Cargo

(1) Imported cargo cannot be unloaded without Customs authority.
(2) If an aircraft is prevented from being taken to an examining station, the goods must be removed from the aircraft to the examining station under the Customs' supervision.
(3) Unless otherwise permitted, all imported goods unloaded from an aircraft are to be deposited forthwith in the transit shed at the airport.

Cargo cannot be loaded for exportation on an aircraft:

(1) until outward clearance has been applied for;
(2) at any place other than the examining station;
(3) without authority of the Customs.

In respect of cargo remaining in transit, the cargo manifest should include the statement 'part cargo remaining on board for exportation'; memorise this phrase.

Health

Passengers entering the UK may be examined medically when suspected of suffering from infectious disease. Persons leaving the UK may be examined when suspected of suffering from quarantinable disease. International certificate of smallpox vaccination is necessary in the case of persons entering the UK from certain countries. People who do not have such a certificate may be offered vaccination and may be put under surveillance or in isolation.

Customs aerodromes

The Customs service provided at an aerodrome is according to the regular traffic needs and season and may be:

(1) Customs is in attendance at all times, or
(2) Customs is in attendance during the normal working hours on weekdays, other than public holidays. Working hours are published in the AIP (AGA

Section). Outside these hours the Customs service is by prior notice only. There are special arrangements available at certain other aerodromes by prior notice for bona fide business purposes.

Customs and immigration requirements have been relaxed so that aircraft carrying only EC citizens (or non-EC citizens approved in advance) may now use a wide range of UK non-Customs designated licensed aerodromes for direct flights to and from all EC countries. Greater flexibility is being given in respect of prior notice, not least because Customs will not be attending every arrival.

Mammals and rabies

A sternly-worded white AIC warns intending visitors to the British Isles of the severe penalties of a large fine with or without a prison sentence if an attempt is made to import a mammal by any means. To maintain this country's rabies-free status, strict import and quarantine controls apply to animals. No exemptions are made in respect of animals which have been vaccinated against rabies.

16
Air Navigation Order

(PPL and IR students need study only the limited number of Articles specified in the CAP53 syllabus.)

The following is the summary of the ANO, as amended, presented in plain and understandable language. Article and paragraph numbers given in the summary need not be memorised by students. Only those articles and paragraphs which form part of the syllabus are dealt with, and where applicable related to the appropriate Annex. The paragraph numbers are the numbers in the Order itself.

Annex 7 – Aircraft Nationality and Registration Marks

Aircraft to be registered – Article 3
With certain exceptions in respect of gliders and aircraft mainly being flown for test or experimental flying ('B' conditions), aircraft shall not fly in or over the UK unless registered in:

(i)   some part of the Commonwealth, or
(ii) a 'contracting state', or
(iii) some other country having an appropriate agreement with the UK.

Registration of aircraft in UK – Article 4 and Schedules 1, 2 and 3
(6) This states that a written application must be made to CAA for an aircraft to be registered in the UK, including evidence of the aircraft, its ownership and any chartering of the aircraft. It particularly emphasises that a proper description must be given according to the 'General Classification of Aircraft' set out in Schedule 1 Part A of the ANO.

(10) If after it has been UK-registered, an unqualified person becomes owner or part-owner of an aircraft the registration becomes void and the Certificate of Registration must be returned to the CAA.

(11) A registered owner must tell the CAA if:
   (a) there is any change in the information provided to the CAA, as in (6) above;
   (b) the aircraft is destroyed or permanently withdrawn from use;
   (c) the demise charter is ended.

(12) Any person who becomes owner of a UK-registered aircraft shall so notify the CAA in writing within 28 days.

(13) The CAA may, if it thinks fit, amend the registration particulars of an aircraft and has power to cancel the registration of an aircraft of which it is satisfied there has been a change of ownership.

Annex 8 – Airworthiness of Aircraft

Certificate of airworthiness – Article 7
(1) An aircraft is prohibited from flying unless it has a valid Certificate of Airworthiness or is making a flight totally within the UK if it is a kite, balloon (not being used for public transport of passengers), glider (not being used for public transport of passengers or for aerial work) or an aircraft flying under a 'Permit to Fly' or 'A' or 'B' conditions for test or experimental flying.
(2) For a UK-registered aircraft, the C of A is issued or validated in accordance with the provisions of Article 8 of the ANO.

Issue of C of A – Article 8
(2) Each C of A will specify the category appropriate to that aircraft and it may only be flown for such purposes (Schedule 3). The categories and purposes specified in Schedule 3 are:

Transport category (Passenger):	Any purpose
Transport category (Cargo):	Any purpose, other than public transport of passengers
Aerial work category:	Any purpose other than public transport
Private category:	Any purpose other than public transport or aerial work
Special category:	Any purpose, other than public transport, specified in the C of A but not including the carriage of passengers unless expressly permitted.

Certificate of Maintenance Review – Article 9
(1) This article applies only to UK-registered aircraft, and of these aircraft only those which are engaged on public transport work or aerial work. Such aircraft are prohibited to fly unless:
   (i) the aircraft and its equipment (including radio) are maintained according to approved schedule,
   (ii) a certificate of maintenance review is in force.
(2) The maintenance schedule must specify when a review must be carried out for the purpose of issuing a certificate of maintenance review.
(3) A certificate of maintenance review can only be issued by a licensed aircraft maintenance engineer or other CAA-authorised person.
(4) An authorised person must verify before issuing a certificate of maintenance

review that the appropriate maintenance and inspections have been carried out, any defects entered in the technical log have been rectified and certificates of release to service have been issued.
(5) A certificate of maintenance review is issued in duplicate, one copy retained by the operator, the other carried in the aircraft if it is a public transport or aerial work flight.
(6) A certificate of maintenance review must be retained for two years.

Technical log – Article 10

(1) A technical log must be kept for any UK-registered aircraft which has a valid C of A in either the transport or the aerial work category.
(2) At the end of every flight made by an aircraft required to carry a technical log, the aircraft commander shall enter in the technical log:
   (i)   the times when the aircraft took-off and landed; and
   (ii) particulars of any defect or if there are no defects, 'no defects'; and
   (iii) any other particulars regarding airworthiness or operation of the aircraft required by the CAA.

If the aircraft MTWA does not exceed 2730 kg and it is not operated by the holder of an air operator's certificate, the entries must be made in any other CAA-approved record which the aircraft commander must also date and sign.

In the case of several consecutive flights on the same day, under the same commander, the entries may be made at the end of the last flight, if a defect did not occur during an earlier flight. If these consecutive flights are for the purpose of public transport, this concession applies only if the flights begin and end at the same aerodrome. This article does not apply to aircraft in the Special Category.

Technical logs or alternative approved records must be preserved until a date 2 years after the aircraft to which it relates has been destroyed or permanently withdrawn from use (or shorter time if CAA permits in a particular case).

The definition of '*Commander*' in relation to an aircraft means the member of the flight crew designated as commander of that aircraft by the operator thereof, or, failing such a designation, the person who is for the time being the pilot in command of the aircraft.

The term '*pilot in command*' is defined as a person who for the time being is in charge of the piloting of the aircraft without being under the direction of any other pilot in the aircraft (see also Article 19).

From the two foregoing definitions, a commander need not necessarily be the person who holds the control column; he is the one who is either so designated, or falls within definition of the 'pilot in command'.

Inspection, overhaul, repair, replacement and modification – Article 11

(1) An aircraft is prohibited from flying if any part or equipment necessary for the Airworthiness of the aircraft has been overhauled, inspected, repaired, replaced or modified, until a certificate of release to service has been issued.
   However, if the inspection, overhaul, repair, etc, was carried out at a place where either this could not be done in a manner qualifying for the certificate

of release to service, or at a place where such a certificate cannot be granted, then the aircraft may fly to a place where the certificate may be granted. When undertaking such a flight:

(i) the pilot must take into consideration such factors as flight safety, equipment availability, liberty and health of any person on board, and

(ii) report the circumstances of the flight to the CAA within 10 days of the flight.

(A light aircraft not exceeding 2730 kg will not be prevented from flying under the conditions of this paragraph, if certain repairs or replacements have been carried out personally by the aircraft's owner or operator if he has a valid pilot's licence.)

(5) 'Certificate of Release to Service' means a certificate that the part of the aircraft or its equipment has been overhauled, repaired, replaced or modified as the case may be, in a manner and with materials of a type approved by the Authority.

(6)(e) In relation only to the adjustment and compensation of direct reading magnetic compasses, the holder of an ATPL (Aeroplanes), a SCPL (aeroplanes) or a Flight Navigator's Licence granted or rendered valid under the Order may issue a Certificate of Release to Service.

Equipment of aircraft – Article 13 and Schedule 4

(1)(i) To comply with the requirement of equipment to be carried on the aircraft, an aircraft must obey the law of the country it is registered in.

(ii) For the purposes of the rules of lights, markings to be displayed and the signals to be made, it must comply with this Order.

Rules of the Air Regulations made under the provisions of the ANO and containing rules of lights, etc, are applicable to:

(a) UK-registered aircraft anywhere in the world, and

(b) aircraft of any country, while in the UK.

(2) For UK-registered aircraft, equipment is required to be provided in accordance with Schedule 4 of the ANO, of an approved type and installed in an approved manner. The pages of Schedule 4 run into double figures and all pilots, both private and professional, are required to know the contents.

Radio equipment of aircraft – Article 14 and Schedule 5

Aircraft must comply with the requirements laid down in the Air Navigation Order. To enable communication to be made and aircraft to be navigated, aircraft registered anywhere also comply with the Order when flying within UK airspace.

Minimum equipment requirements – Article 15

With CAA's permission, an aircraft may start a specified flight even if all the equipment required by the ANO is not being carried or is unserviceable. The aircraft commander has to satisfy himself that either he can meet the conditions in the CAA's permission or that all the required equipment is being carried and is serviceable.

Aircraft, engine and propeller log books – Article 16

(1) For UK-registered aircraft, there must be kept:

    (i)   an aircraft log book, and

    (ii) a log book for each engine fitted in the aircraft, and

    (iii) a separate log book for each variable pitch propeller fitted to the aircraft.

For aircraft of MTWA not exceeding 2730 kg, the log book must be CAA-approved.

(2) Each entry must be made as soon as possible and in no event more than 7 days after the Certificate of Maintenance Review expires.

(3) If other documents are referred to in the log book, they must be clearly identified and become part of the log book as far as the ANO is concerned.

(4) (5) It is the duty of the operator to see that log books are properly kept and to preserve the log books until a date 2 years after the aircraft, engine or propeller has been destroyed or withdrawn from use.

Aircraft Weight Schedule – Article 17

(1) Every flying machine or glider with a valid C of A must be weighed and its centre of gravity (CG) determined as required by the CAA.

(2) After weighing, the operator must prepare a weight schedule to show either the basic weight of the aircraft (empty weight + weight of unusable fuel and oil in the aircraft + such items stated in the weight schedule) or such other weight approved by the CAA; and either the CG position at the basic weight or at the other weight approved by the CAA.

(3) Normally the weight schedule must be preserved by the operator for 6 months after the next occasion that the aircraft is weighed.

Annex 1 – Personnel licensing

Composition of crew of aircraft – Article 19

(1) Minimum crew of any aircraft should be as laid down in the law of the country of registration.

(2) to (8) For UK-registered aircraft the following rules apply:

    (i)   The aircraft must carry adequate crew (in number and description), or at least that specified in the C of A.

    (ii)   A public transport flying machine of maximum total weight authorised (MTWA) of more than 5700 kg must carry a crew of at least two pilots.

    (iii) With effect from 1 January 1990 public transport aeroplanes of MTWA

5700 kg or less, under IFR must carry two pilots if they are multi-engined or powered by turbine jet or powered by one or more turbo-prop engines and pressurised. (Unpressurised turbo-prop aircraft which may only carry less than 10 passengers, and piston engined aircraft, may carry only one pilot provided that the aircraft has a serviceable approved auto-pilot.)

(iv) When the route, or diversion as planned, exceeds a distance of 500 nm from the take-off point and part of the route passes over any part of the area described in Schedule 7 of the Order (you need not study the details), then that aircraft should carry a flight navigator or navigation equipment approved by the CAA. This rule only applies to public transport aircraft.

(The equipping of aircraft with modern navigation triplicated systems has led to the phasing out of flight navigators. There is usually at least one yellow AIC current on MNPS – minimum navigation performance specifications.)

(v) Where an aircraft is required to carry radio equipment in accordance with Article 14 and the nature of the flight calls for operation of radio telegraph apparatus (W/T), a flight radio operator must be carried as an additional crew member.

(vi) The CAA may direct any operator to allocate additional persons to act as members of flight crew.

(vii) For public transport flights, cabin attendants separate from the members of the flight crew must be carried for safety duties when:
   - carrying 20 or more passengers (PAX)
   - carrying at least 1 passenger if the C of A permits the carriage of more than 35 PAX.

The number of cabin attendants is one for every 50 (or fraction of 50) PAX seats installed in the aircraft. The CAA can grant written permission for an operator to carry less than the calculated number for a particular flight but equally can require operators to carry extra cabin attendants to the calculated number.

Crew Member – definition. Every person employed or engaged in an aircraft in flight on the business of the aircraft shall be deemed to be a member of the crew thereof.

Flight Crew – definition. Flight crew in relation to an aircraft means those members of the crew of the aircraft who respectively undertake to act as pilot, flight navigator, flight engineer or flight radio operator of the aircraft.

Co-pilot – definition. Co-pilot in relation to an aircraft means a pilot, who in performing his duties as such, is subject to the direction of another pilot carried in the aircraft.

Members of flight crew – Licences – Article 20

(1) The general rule is that a person shall not act as a member of the flight crew

of an aircraft registered in the UK unless he is the holder of an appropriate licence. The following exceptions should be noted:

(i) A glider pilot (not flying for the purpose of public transport or aerial work) or a person being trained in an aircraft may act as flight radio telephony operator without being the holder of such a licence if certain conditions are met. One of the conditions is that he is authorised to operate RTF by another person who is a holder of such a licence, and that the RTF is used only for the purpose of instruction or safety or navigation of the aircraft.

(ii) A person may act as pilot in command without possessing a licence provided he is training to be qualified for the grant or renewal of a pilot's licence, he is at least 17 years of age and holds a valid medical certificate. He must be authorised by a flying instructor (QFI) or assistant flying instructor and cannot carry any passengers. The aircraft used must fly in an instructional role only.

(iii) A person may also act as pilot in command, when either flying in a dual control aircraft when accompanied by, and receiving instruction from, a QFI or when night flying under instruction by a QFI. Similarly a pilot in command of a balloon is permitted when a CAA-authorised person is giving instruction in the balloon.

(6) A person may act as a flight crew member of a UK-registered aircraft without holding the appropriate licence if, in so doing, he is acting in the course of his duties as a member of any of HM armed services.

Grant and renewal of licences to members of flight crew – Article 21

(a) A licence holder is entitled to perform the functions specified in the Order in respect of that licence. Similarly a rating of any class entitles the holder of the licence to perform the functions specified in the Order in respect of that rating. The privileges attached to a licence or rating may not be exercised in the following circumstances:

(i) If he does not have the appropriate rating, except when under training. Night rating is required in the case of a private pilot or a basic commercial pilot.

(ii) When a person knows or believes his physical or mental condition to be such as to render him temporarily or permanently unfit to perform his duties, he must report the matter to the CAA and consider his licence suspended. And for a female member of flight crew, pregnancy automatically suspends the holder's licence.

(iii) If the licence does not include a valid medical certificate, he cannot exercise the privilege. This rule does not apply to RTF licence holders.

(iv) If the licence does not bear a valid certificate of test, or a valid certificate of experience, the privilege cannot be exercised. *This means that failure to pass a renewal test invalidates the licence.*

(v) If the following tests are not complete and the licence does not bear a signed certificate to that effect, the privilege cannot be exercised:
Instrument Rating – test inside 13 months – flight test: this applies to aeroplanes and helicopters.

Assistant Flight Instructor Rating – test inside 13 months – flight test. Flying Instructor Rating and Instrument Meteorological Conditions Rating (aeroplanes) – test inside 25 months – flight test.

The Instrument Rating test may be carried out on a flight simulator approved by the CAA.

(b) The licence must be signed in ink upon receipt.

(c) Medical examination is required for all licences except the RTF licence.

(d) The medical certificate forms part of the licence. It is valid for the period specified in the certificate, subject to:
  (i) remaining fit during that period, and
  (ii) not becoming pregnant.

(e) All licence holders, except RTF operators, must inform the CAA in writing in case of any injury or illness as follows:
  (i) personal injury – as soon as possible;
  (ii) illness – after a period of 20 days has elapsed. Thus, if you are unfit to fly due to a cold, you have 20 days to recover in. If still unfit, you must report on the 21st day.

(f) When the above mentioned report has been made, the licence is deemed to be suspended until either a new, satisfactory medical examination takes place, or an exemption from such examination is granted by the CAA.

(g) In the case of pregnancy, the suspension may be lifted by the Authority for such period and subject to such conditions as it thinks fit, otherwise a licence remains invalid until the pregnancy has ended and the person is pronounced medically fit.

(h) A Flight Navigator Licence holder must have an appropriate certificate of experience if he is to carry out duties on a flight for which the ANO lays down that a flight navigator must be carried. Similarly, a PPL-holder may not exercise the privileges of an aircraft rating specified in the licence unless the personal log book contains a relevant certificate of test or experience.

(i) The CAA may, with or without conditions, approve:

  (a) any course of training or instruction;
  (b) a person to provide any course of training or instruction;
  (c) a person as qualified to furnish reports to it and accept such reports and the CAA may authorise a person to conduct such examinations or tests as it may specify.

Flight crew licences and ratings – Schedule 8

Private Pilot's Licence (Aeroplanes)

Minimum age: 17 years

No maximum period of validity.

Privileges: Can fly as pilot in command or co-pilot of the types and rating given in the licence provided that:

(a) he cannot fly an aeroplane for public transport or aerial work except for aerial work consisting of:

     (i)   giving flying instruction (if his licence includes a FI or AFI rating) or conducting flying tests through club arrangements,

     (ii) and similarly towing a glider or dropping parachutists;

(b) he cannot receive remuneration as a pilot except for instruction or testing in microlights or self-launching gliders;

(c) unless his licence includes an Instrument Rating (aeroplanes) (IR) or an Instrument Meteorological Conditions Rating (aeroplanes) (IMC) he cannot fly as pilot in command

     (i)   on a flight outside controlled airspace notified for this purpose when:
- flight visibility is less than 3 km or
- any passenger is carried and the aeroplane is either flying above 3000 ft amsl in such conditions that it cannot remain at least 1800 m horizontally and 1000 ft vertically from cloud and in a flight visibility of at least 10 km, or at or below 3000 ft amsl in a flight visibility of less than 5 km;

     (ii) on a Special VFR Flight in a control zone in a flight visibility of less than 10 km except if on a notified route or in a notified ATZ;

     (iii) out of sight of the surface,

(d) cannot fly at night as pilot in command unless his licence includes a night rating and an IR (aeroplanes) or he has within the immediately preceding 13 months carried out as pilot in command not less than 5 take-offs and 5 landings at a time when the depression of the sun's centre was not less than 12 degrees below the horizon.

(e) unless his licence includes an IR (aeroplanes) he cannot fly as pilot in command or as co-pilot on a flight in airspace notified for this purpose:

     (i)   in conditions such that he cannot comply with the specified minimum weather conditions or

     (ii) in circumstances requiring compliance with IFR.

Basic Commercial Pilots Licence (Aeroplanes)

Minimum Age: 18 years

Maximum period of validity: 10 years

Privileges: (1) as per private pilot (aeroplanes) and (2) can fly in command of a type specified in Part 1 of the aircraft rating in the licence for any purpose provided that he shall *not* fly:

(a) for public transport if he has less than 400 hours flying experience as pilot in command (ignoring microlights and self launching motor gliders);

(b) for public transport if the MTWA exceeds 2300 kg;

(c) on a scheduled journey;

(d) for public transport except for a flight beginning and ending at the same aerodrome and not beyond 25 nm from that aerodrome;

(e) for public transport after he is 60 years old unless the aeroplane has dual controls and carries another pilot under 60 years old who has an appropriate licence entitling him to act as pilot in command or co-pilot on the aeroplane;

(f) at night, unless he has a night rating and his licence includes an IR or he has within the immediately preceding 13 months carried out as pilot in command at least five take-offs and five landings when the depression of the sun's centre is not less than 12° below the horizon, ie. when it's dark;

(g) unless he has an IR or an IMC rating, as pilot in command:

    (i) on a flight outside controlled airspace notified for this schedule when:

- the flight visibility is less than 3 km or
- any passenger is carried and the aeroplane is flying either above 3000 ft amsl in such conditions that it cannot remain at least 1800 m horizontally and 1000 ft vertically from cloud and in flight visibility of at least 10 km, or at or below 3000 ft amsl in a flight visibility of less than 5 km;

    (ii) on a Special VFR Flight in a control zone in a flight visibility of less than 10 km except if on a notified route or in a notified ATZ;

    (iii) out of sight of the surface.

(h) unless licence includes an IR (aeroplanes), as pilot in command or as a co-pilot on a flight in airspace notified for this purpose:

    (i) in conditions such that he cannot comply with the specified minimum weather conditions or

    (ii) in circumstances requiring compliance with IFR.

(3) Can fly in command of a type specified in any FI or AFI rating for aerial work consisting of giving flying instruction or conducting flying tests. This is subject also to the conditions that (a) he is entitled to fly the aircraft under his private privileges and (b) the instruction is carried out under flying club auspices of which the instructor and the pupil are members.

(4) Can fly as co-pilot on any aircraft specified in the rating on his licence when flying for any purpose whatsoever provided that it is not public transport unless he has more than 400 hours as pilot in command (ignoring microlights and self launching motor gliders) and the aeroplane's MTWA does not exceed 5700 kg* (see below).

(5) *Cannot* fly as pilot in command or co-pilot of any aeroplane for public transport after reaching 65 years of age.

Commercial Pilot's Licence
Minimum age: 18 years
Maximum validity: 10 years
Privileges:

(1) as per a private pilot with an IMC and night rating, and can fly in command:

    (a) on a special VFR flight even if flight visibility is less than 3 km;

    (b) on take-off and landing despite flight visibility below cloud being less than 1800 m.

(2) Can fly in command of an aeroplane specified in Part I of the aircraft rating included in the licence when the aircraft is flying for any purpose whatsoever, *but not:*

    (a) on a scheduled journey unless he has an Instrument Rating (aeroplanes);

    (b) at night, unless he has an IR or has during the immediately preceding 13 months carried out as pilot in command not less than 5 take-offs and 5 landings when the depression of the sun's centre is not less than 12 degrees below the horizon;

(c) unless he has an Instrument Rating, an aircraft of MTWA of more than 2300 kg on a flight for public transport, except one beginning and ending at the same aerodrome, and not beyond 25 nm from that aerodrome;

(d) an aircraft of MTWA of more than 5700 kg* (see below) on a flight for public transport;

(e) a public transport aeroplane when he is 60 years old unless the aeroplane has dual controls and carries another pilot under 60 years old who has an appropriate licence entitling him to act as pilot-in-command or co-pilot on the aeroplane;

(f) unless he has an Instrument Rating, fly as pilot in command or as co-pilot in airspace notified for the purpose of this Schedule:
  (i) in conditions that he cannot comply with the specified minimum weather provisions or
  (ii) in conditions requiring compliance with IFR.

(3) Can fly as pilot in command of an aeroplane type specified in any FI or AFI rating for aerial work consisting of giving flying instruction or conducting flight tests. This is subject also to the conditions that:
  (a) he is entitled to fly the aircraft under the private, aerial work or public transport privileges, and
  (b) the instruction is carried out under flying club auspices of which the instructor and the pupil(s) are members.

(4) Can fly as co-pilot on any aircraft specified in the rating on his licence when flying for any purpose whatsoever, provided that he may not after reaching 60 years of age act as co-pilot of any aeroplane over 20 000 kg MTWA flying for public transport.

(5) Cannot fly as pilot-in-command or co-pilot of any aeroplane flying for public transport after attaining 65 years of age.

* After 3 December 1994, instead of MTWA 5700 kg a new criterion of whether the aircraft is certificted for single pilot operation will apply. Newly-issued BCPLs and CPLs allow this privilege with immediate effect.

Senior Commercial Pilot's Licence
As CPL except minimum age 21 and 2(d) substitute 20 000 kg for 5700 kg. No new SCPLs are being granted and current SCPLs will expire on or before 3 December 1994.

Airline Transport Pilot's Licence
Minimum age: 21 years
Maximum validity: 10 years
Privileges: as for the Commercial Pilot's Licence, except that for proviso (d) to paragraph 2 shall be substituted:
(d) never after he has reached 60 years of age, such an aeroplane for public transport if its MTWA exceeds 20 000 kg as pilot-in-command or as co-pilot.

Commercial Pilot's Licence (helicopters and gyroplanes)
Minimum age: 18 years
Maximum validity: 10 years
Privileges:
(1) as for a Private Pilot (Helicopters and Gyroplanes) with the appropriate night rating.
(2) as pilot in command of a helicopter or gyroplane specified in Part I of the rating included in the licence on a flight for any purpose whatsoever, *but not:*
   (a) unless he has got an Instrument Rating (helicopters), on any scheduled journey or for public transport if he cannot comply with the specified minimum weather conditions;
   (b) for public transport, if MTWA exceeds 5700 kg;
   (c) a gyroplane at night unless he has done the lot on 2(b) CPL above;
   (d) ditto helicopter, unless he has an Instrument Rating (helicopters) or he has within the immediately preceding 13 months carried out as pilot in command not less than 5 flights, each consisting of a take-off, a transition from hover to forward flight, a climb to at least 500 ft, and a landing at a time when the depression of the sun's centre was not less than 12° below the horizon;
   (e) unless he has an Instrument Rating (helicopters), fly as pilot in comand or as co-pilot in airspace notified for the purpose of this schedule:
      (i) in conditions that he cannot comply with the specified minimum weather provisions, or
      (ii) in conditions requiring compliance with IFR.
(3) Can fly as co-pilot of any helicopter or gyroplane specified in Part I of the aircraft rating on the licence on a flight for any purpose whatsoever. However, he may not fly as co-pilot of any helicopter or gyroplane of MTWA exceeding 20 000 kg for any public transport flight after attaining the age of 60 years.
(4) Cannot fly as pilot-in-command or as co-pilot of any helicopter or gyroplane flying for public transport after attaining 65 years of age.

Airline Transport Pilot's Licence (helicopters and gyroplanes)
Minimum age: 21 years
Maximum validity: 10 years
Privileges: as for the Commercial Licence (Helicopters and Gyroplanes) except proviso (b) to paragraph 2 does not apply, i.e. he can fly a helicopter or gyroplane whose MTWA is more than 5700 kg. After attaining the age of 60 years, he cannot act as pilot-in-command or co-pilot of any helicopter or gyroplane flying for public transport if MTWA exceeds 20 000 kg.

NB: In June 1988 CAA announced that with immediate effect, all applicants for a professional pilot's licence must have satisfactorily completed a recognised course of night flying training.

Ratings
Aircraft ratings: the pilot may fly the aircraft specified in the aircraft rating on the licence:

Instrument rating (aeroplanes or helicopters): the pilot may fly in controlled airspace notified for the purpose of this schedule in conditions in which he cannot comply with the specified minimum weather conditions or in IFR, in command or as co-pilot.

Flying instructor's rating: may give instruction of types of aircraft specified on the rating.

Assistant flying instructor's rating: may give instruction in flying *but*
(a) a qualified flying instructor must be present to supervise his instruction during take-off and landing;
(b) he may not offer any advice or directions to a pupil about his first solo, his first solo at night, his first solo cross-country by day and by night.

IMC Rating (Aeroplanes): PPL or BCPL holder may fly as pilot in command without being subject to certain provisos on the licence privileges, provided he does not fly:
(a) on a special VFR flight in a Control Zone in a flight visibility of less than 3 km;
(b) when the aeroplane is taking off or landing at any place if the flight visibility below cloud is lesss than 1800 m.

*Validation of licences – Article 22
Subject to any conditions and period of time that the CAA thinks fit, the CAA may issue a certificate of validation to a non-UK issued licence for a member of flight crew.

Personal flying log books – Article 23
(1) A personal flying log book must be maintained by every member of the flight crew, and by every person who flies for the purpose of qualifying for the initial grant or renewal of a licence, or taking a test or receiving instruction. The following particulars are recorded:
   (a) the name and address of the holder;
   (b) particulars of holder's licence to act as a member of the flight crew;
   (c) the name and address of his employer (if any).
(2) Particulars of each flight made by the holder of the log book must be made immediately or as soon as practicable after landing, including:
   (a) date, places of embarkation and disembarkation, and the times during the flight that he was acting as a crew member or flying for the purpose of grant or renewal of a licence;
   (b) the type and registration marks of the aircraft;
   (c) the capacity in which the holder acted in flight;
   (d) particulars of any special conditions, including night flying and instrument flying;
   (e) particulars of any test or examination undertaken whilst in flight.

(3) A helicopter is deemed to be in flight from the moment it first moves under its own power for the purpose of taking-off until the rotors are next stopped.

(4) Particulars of any test or examination taken in a flight simulator shall be recorded in the log book, including:
   (a) the date of the test or examination;
   (b) the type of simulator;
   (c) the capacity in which the holder acted;
   (d) the nature of the test or examination.

Instruction in flying – Article 24

(1) A pilot shall not give flying instruction unless he has a valid licence to act as pilot in command of the aircraft and for the circumstances of the instruction, together with a flying instructor's or assistant flying instructor's rating.

(2) The article applies to any flying instruction for the purpose of qualifying for a pilot's licence or the inclusion or variation of any rating in his licence. It does not apply to flights for the inclusion in the licence of a rating to act as pilot of a multi-engine aircraft if that person has had a previous entitlement or been a service pilot of that class of aircraft.

**Operations manual – Article 26*

(1) This article applies to all UK registered public transport aircraft, except when on a flight of less than 60 minutes' duration for either of the following purposes:
   (i) training;
   (ii) any purpose, provided the flight begins and ends at the same aerodrome.

(2) The operator should maintain an Operations Manual up-to-date and make it available to the operations staff. The crew should have access to the relevant parts of it in flight. The manual should contain all relevant information and instructions, and, in particular, that laid down in Part A of Schedule 10 of the Order including, for example, information and instructions on the carriage of dangerous goods. (See also Article 47.)

   However, any such information which is included in flight manual need not be repeated in the operations manual.

**Training manual – Article 27*

(1) For every UK-registered aircraft flying for public transport, the operator must ensure that a training manual is kept up-to-date and made available to every person appointed by the operator to give or supervise training, experience, practice or periodical tests required by the ANO.

**Public transport – operator's responsibilities – Article 28*

(1) The operator of a UK-registered aircraft shall not permit it to fly for the purpose of public transport without first:
   (a) designating from the flight crew a pilot to be the aircraft commander for the flight; and

(b) checking that the radio and navigational aids for the route and any diversion are adequate for safe navigation; and

(c) checking that all aerodromes likely to be used are properly manned and equipped to ensure the safety of the aircraft and its passengers.

(2) Except for flight crew training, the operator of a UK-registered aircraft operating for the purpose of public transport may not allow a person to carry out flight crew duties unless that person is licensed, competent and able to use the aircraft equipment and must keep evidence to this effect.

(3) The operator of a UK-registered aircraft on a public transport flight shall not permit simulated emergency procedures which could adversely affect the flight characteristics of the aircraft.

Loading – Article 29 and Air Navigation (General) Regulations 4 and 5

(1) Loading shall be carried out for the purpose of public transport only under supervision. The supervising person should have written instructions as to the distribution and securing of the load. This is to ensure that:

(i) the load is carried safely, and

(ii) conditions of the certificate of airworthiness are complied with.

(4) The supervising person will prepare and sign the load sheet in duplicate, and the commander of the aircraft will thereafter examine and sign it. The rule given in this paragraph does not apply when:

(i) the load, distribution and securing remain unchanged upon the next flight, provided the commander has so endorsed the load sheet on the previous flight, or

(ii) the aircraft is exempted under Article 29(2) (the provisions of this paragraph are not in your syllabus).

(5) One copy of the load sheet will be carried in the aircraft, except when:

(i) the flight begins and ends at the same place, and

(ii) the flight path does not take the aircraft over any territory other than the UK.

In these circumstances, the load sheet may be kept at the aerodrome.

The duplicate and the instructions are preserved for six months. The Article applies to UK registered aircraft only.

In the exercise of this Article further regulations are promulgated in the Air Navigation (General) Regulations. These lay down the following:

(a) Every load sheet shall contain the following particulars:

(i)   the nationality mark of the aircraft and its registration mark;

(ii) particulars of the flight to which the load sheet relates;

(iii) the total weight of the aircraft as loaded for that flight;

(iv) weights of the several items from which the total weight of the aircraft has been calculated, including, in particular, the weight of the aircraft prepared for service, respective total weights of the passengers, crew, baggage and cargo carried in flight;

(v)   the manner in which the load is distributed and the resulting position of the centre of gravity.

At the foot, the loading supervisor shall sign a certificate that the aircraft has been loaded in accordance with the written instructions furnished to him by the operator.

(b) The total weight of the passengers, crew and the baggage is to be computed from the actual weights. However, in the case of an aircraft having a total seating capacity of 12 or more, or having its total weight authorised exceeding 5700 kg, all these items may be calculated as follows, and the load sheet shall bear a notation to this effect:

Passengers and crew:

Females over 12 years of age	65 kg
Males over 12 years of age (except for *)	75 kg
* Males over 12 years, in helicopters over seas around UK	83 kg

On journeys between the UK, the CI and IoM

Children aged 3 to 12 (both inc.)	40 kg
Infants under 3	10 kg

On any other journey

Children aged 2 to 12 (both inc.)	39 kg
Infants under 2	8 kg

Baggage and cargo:

Cabin baggage per passenger is 3 kg. Hold baggage per piece is as follows:

Domestic route	10 kg if it is a scheduled journey
	13 kg if it is a holiday journey
European route	12 kg and 13 kg respectively
Intercontinental route	14 kg and 16 kg respectively

The loading supervisor, however, has authority to have any individual passenger or baggage actually weighed if he considers it necessary in the interests of the safety of the aircraft. In any case where an individual or his baggage is actually weighed this weight is compared with the weight allowed in the regulations above, and the higher weight of the two is entered in the load sheet.

*Public transport: operating conditions – Article 30

(1) Aircraft must comply with requirements in respect of weight and related performance, except when on training.

(2) Assessment of weight and performance are to be based on information in the Certificate of Airworthiness. Where this information is insufficient, the commander may base the assessment on best available information.

(3) When flying over water, a public transport aircraft shall fly at such height that in the event of one engine failure it could reach a place where landing may be made with safety.

(4) A single or a twin engine public transport aircraft shall not fly more than 60 minutes' flying time from the nearest coastline, if that aircraft is in performance group X.

(5) (a) A helicopter, whose Certificate of Airworthiness designates it as being Group B, shall not fly over water for the purpose of public transport for

more than 20 seconds from whence it can make an autorotative descent to land in emergency unless equipped with CAA approved apparatus to land on water – and then not for more than 3 minutes unless permitted in writing by the Authority and all its conditions are complied with.

(6) If a helicopter is designated as Group A2, it shall not fly over water for the purpose of public transport for more than 15 minutes unless equipped with approved apparatus to land safely on water.

The flying time here is calculated as flying in still air at the speed specified in the Certificate of Airworthiness as the speed for compliance with the regulations governing flights over water.

Aerodrome operating minima – Article 31

This article applies to public transport aircraft, unless for flights not exceeding 60 minutes which are either solely for training persons for duties in the aircraft, or flights intended to begin and end at the same aerodrome.

(4) An aircraft shall not commence a flight when:
   (a) the cloud ceiling or the runway visual range at the departure aerodrome is less than the relevant specified minimum for take-off, or
   (b) when from information available to the commander it could not commence or continue an approach to landing at the intended destination at ETA, and at any alternative aerodrome at any time the aircraft might reasonably expect to arrive there.

(5) An aircraft when making a descent to an aerodrome shall not descend below 1000 ft above the height of the aerodrome if the relevant RVR at the aerodrome is at the time less than the specified minimum for landing.

(6) An aircraft when making a descent to an aerodrome shall not:
   (i) continue an approach to landing at any aerodrome by flying below the relevant specified decision height, or
   (ii) descend below the relevant specified minimum descent height unless from that height, the specified visual reference for landing is established and maintained.

(7) If the aircraft be required to fly in IFR at the aerodrome of intended landing, the commander shall, prior to take-off, select an alternative aerodrome, unless no such suitable aerodrome is available.

(8) 'Specified' means specified by the operator in the operations manual relating to that aircraft or given in writing to the aircraft commander.

Approach to landing means that portion of the flight of the aircraft in which it is descending below a height of 1000 ft above the decision height or the minimum descent height.

Decision height is a specified height at which missed approach must be initiated if the required visual reference to continue the approach to land has not been established. This is specified in the operations manual, and takes into consideration OCH(A), aircraft performance and approach and missed approach systems.

Minimum descent height (MDH) is the height in a non-precision approach below which descent may not be made without the required visual reference.

The *take-off and landing minima* are prescribed in terms of:
(i)   cloud ceiling and RVR for take-off, and
(ii) decision height, RVR, and visual reference for landing.

Cloud ceiling in relation to an aerodrome means the vertical distance from the elevation of the aerodrome to the lowest part of any cloud visible from the aerodrome which is sufficient to obscure more than one-half of the sky so visible.

The actual minima in the above terms are normally published in the operations manual, approved by the CAA, and a pilot cannot take-off or land when the weather conditions are less than the prescribed minima.

Pre-flight action by commander of aircraft – Article 35
Applies to the commander of a UK registered aircraft only.
(i)   Ensure that the flight can safely be made, taking into consideration weather forecast for the route and any alternate course of action.
(ii)   Ensure that the equipment is in fit condition. (See Article 14 for certain exemptions applicable to permission for a specific flight.)
(iii) Ensure that aircraft is in every way fit for the intended flight.
(iv)   Ensure that Certificate of maintenance review is valid, and will remain valid throughout the flight.
(v)   Check load for weight, distribution and security.
(vi)   Check that sufficient fuel, oil and engine coolant are carried on the flight for all contingencies. In case of a public transport, the instructions in the operations manual shall be complied with.
(vii) In the case of airship or balloon, check that sufficient ballast is carried.
(viii) In the case of a flying machine, having regard to the performance of the aircraft, check that it is capable of safely taking off, reaching and maintaining a safe height thereafter, and making a safe landing, in the conditions expected, and with regard to any obstructions anywhere on the trip.
(ix)   Ensure that any pre-flight check system laid down by the operator and set out in the operations manual or elsewhere has been complied with by each crew member.

Passenger briefing by commander – Article 36
The commander of an aircraft flying for any purpose must before take-off brief any passengers being carried as to the position and method of use of safety equipment carried in the aircraft and action which should be taken by passengers in an emergency.

Pilots to remain at controls – wearing survival suits – Articles 33 and 34
This article applies to UK registered aircraft only.
(i)   Any flying machine or glider: at least one pilot must remain at the controls at all times.
(ii) If the aircraft is required under provisions of the Order to carry two pilots, both pilots are to remain at the controls during take-off and landing. If,

however, the aircraft is engaged on a flight for the purpose of the public transport of passengers and carries two or more pilots, the commander himself is to remain at the controls during the take-off and landing.

(iii) Pilots at the controls are to be secured by safety belts or safety harnesses.

(iv) If the aircraft is required to be fitted with safety harnesses, the pilot or pilots at the controls during take-offs and landing are to use safety harnesses.

In Article 34 the crew must wear a survival suit if the Order requires that such a suit must be carried.

Public transport of passengers – duties of the commander – Article 37 and Schedule 4

(1) This article applies to public transport aircraft registered in the UK and lays down the duties of the commander augmenting those laid down in Article 35 as follows:

(2) Check that the passengers are familiar with exits, safety belts and harnesses, oxygen equipment and life jackets (and any other device that the operator might be required to install), before take-off.

The rules regarding familiarisation and demonstration of life jackets depend on whether the aircraft is a land plane or a sea-plane and are given in Fig. 16.1.

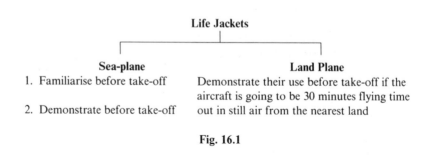

Fig. 16.1

Before take-off and before landing, the crew are to be secured in their seats. Flight attendants are to be seated and secured in the passenger cabin, and are to be available to the passengers.

Before take-off and before landing and during turbulent conditions, or when the conditions so warrant, passengers 2 years old or more are to be secured in their seats. Those under 2 must be properly secured by mens of a child restraint device. The provision of safety belts and harnesses is covered in Schedule 4.

In an emergency, ensure that the passengers are informed of the procedures.

Ensure the security of items of baggage in the passenger compartment which by their size, weight or nature should be secured. If the aircraft can seat more than 30 PAX, such baggage must be secured to seats or in the approved stowage places.

Unless a cabin pressure of greater than 700 mb is maintained throughout the flight, oxygen must be used. The rules for aircraft whose C of A was first issued before 1 January 1989 are as follows:

(i) demonstrate the use of oxygen equipment to the passengers before flight

level 130 is reached. On reaching that altitude, *recommend* its use to the passengers and cabin attendants.
(ii) Crew must remain on oxygen when flying above flight level 130 and oxygen is to be used continuously whenever the flight is above flight level 100.
For aircraft with C of A first issued on or after 1 January 1989, except if more than 700 mb pressure is maintained throughout the flight:
(i)   demonstrate the use of the oxygen equipment to passengers before FL 100 is reached;
(ii) flight crew must remain on oxygen when flying above FL 100;
(iii) recommend all passengers and cabin attendants use oxygen above FL 120.

Operation of Radio in aircraft – Article 38
(1) Radio should be operated only:
  (i) in accordance with the conditions of the licence issued by the country where the aircraft is registered, and
  (ii) by a person duly licensed, or one authorised under this law.
(2) Where a radio is a requisite part of the aircraft's equipment, continuous watch should be maintained on the appropriate frequency or on a frequency requested by the ground station. Listening watch may be discontinued if the ground station permits. Watch may be kept by automatic device (Selcal) as follows:
  (i)   the ground station has been informed of your intentions, and
  (ii) it has raised no objection, and
  (iii) that ground station has been notified as capable of such operation.
  Outside the UK Selcal watch may be maintained only if the ground station concerned is designated as transmitting suitable signals for that purpose.
(3) Operate radio or radio navigation equipment as instructed by ATC or 'as notified'.
(4) Aircraft using radio shall not cause interference and shall not transmit except:
  (i)   on an emission class and frequency appropriate to the airspace the aircraft is flying in;
  (ii) to send distress and urgency and difficulty messages;
  (iii) to send messages relating to flight;
  (iv) to send such public correspondence as is permitted under the licence.
(5) A UK registered aircraft shall maintain a radio log and enter the following entries in it:
  (i)   identification of the aircraft radio statio;
  (ii) date and time of beginning and end of radio watch, frequencies used;
  (iii) date, time and particulars of all messages sent or received including in particular details of distress messages sent or received;
  (iv) action taken on distress messages or signals received;
  (v)   radio failure or other interruption.
  Radio telecommunication log book is not required in the case of RTF transmissions. When kept, radio log books must be retained for 6 months.
(6) The pilot and flight engineer of a UK registered public transport aircraft are

not to use hand held microphones even for intercommunication within the aircraft:
(i)   when taking-off and landing, and
(ii) when flying in controlled airspace below FL 150.

Minimum Navigation Performance (MNP) – Article 39

A UK-registered aircraft cannot fly in airspace laid down pursuant to the ANO unless it has equipment (installed, maintained and operated as approved by CAA) to maintain the prescribed navigation performance capability and so operated when in the specified airspace.

Area navigation equipment (UK Reg. Aircraft) – Article 39A

Certain parts of controlled airspace are notified as area navigation routes or areas. To fly in such routes or areas an aircraft must be equipped with approved area navigation equipment which has been installed and maintained in an approved manner and the aircraft must be navigated by means of that equipment. Apart from those notified area navigation routes or areas within which area is mandatory, certain other parts of controlled airspace are notified for area navigation purposes. Within this additional notified airspace it is not mandatory for aircraft to use area navigation equipment but if it is used, the equipment must be of an approved type, installed and maintained in an approved manner.

Area navigation equipment (non-UK Reg. aircraft) – Article 39B

Similar to Article 39A but the equipment must be approved, installed and maintained in compliance with the law of the country in which the aircraft is registered.

Flight recorders – Article 40

(1) Where required to be carried, a flight data recorder or cockpit voice recorder must be in use from the start of the take-off run to the end of the landing run.
(2) An operator must preserve both the last 25 hours made by the flight data recorder and the record of a complete representative flight made in the last 12 months.
(3) For a helicopter, a cockpit voice recorder must be in use from the time the rotors start turning until they are next stopped and the last 8 hours of the recording preserved.

Towing of gliders – Article 41

(1) The certificate of airworthiness of the towing aircraft issued under the law of the country in which the aircraft is registered must specifically state that the aircraft may be used for towing.
(2) The towing aircraft, rope and glider in flight altogether shall not exceed 150 m.

(3) Before take-off, the commander shall satisfy himself that:
(a) the tow rope condition, strength for the job, conditions of flight, obstructions at departure aerodrome and en route *et alia* are such that the take-off, climb and maintaining a safe height for release can be effected and that the towing aircraft can land safely at the intended destination;
(b) signals have been agreed between people suitably stationed to enable safe take-off;
(c) emergency signals have been agreed between the commanders of the towing aircraft and the glider, to be used by the commander in front to suggest immediate release and by the one behind to indicate that it cannot.
(4) The glider shall be attached to the towing aircraft by means of the tow rope before the aircraft takes off.

Towing, picking up and raising of persons and articles – Article 42

Unless the Certificate of Airworthiness is so endorsed, an aircraft is not permitted to tow any article other than a glider, or pick up or raise any person, animal or article. The picking up or raising is however not prohibited in an emergency or for the purpose of saving life. An aircraft shall not tow any article other than a glider at night or when flight visibility is less than one nm, and the length of the combination shall not exceed 150 metres. An aircraft shall not launch or pick up tow-ropes, banners or similar articles other than at an aerodrome.

A helicopter shall not fly at any height over the congested area of a city, town or settlement at any time when an article, person or animal is suspended therefrom, nor in such a case carry any passenger unless he or she has duties in connection with the article, person or animal or a passenger picked up/raised by external means and who it is intended to be lowered to the surface.

Dropping of animals and articles – Article 43

(1) to (4) Articles and animals are not to be dropped or permitted to be dropped so as to endanger persons or property. Over UK territory articles and animals are not to be dropped whether attached to parachute or not, except in the following circumstances:
(i) to save life;
(ii) jettisoning of fuel and other articles in emergency;
(iii) the dropping of ballast in the form of fine sand or water;
(iv) dropping of articles solely for navigational purposes;
(v) dropping of ropes, banners or similar articles at an aerodrome in accordance with prescribed regulations;
(vi) for public health purposes or as a measure against weather conditions, surface icing or oil pollution or training for such dropping, in accordance with any conditions under which it is permitted;
(vii) dropping of wind drift indicators to enable parachute descents, subject to CAA permission and any conditions imposed.

Although the law on the matter is as stated above, a machinery exists whereby an 'exemption' or 'permission' is occasionally granted for an aircraft to drop any article, person or animal (including tow ropes or banners other than at an aerodrome in accordance with prescribed regulation) or for parachuting. Articles may be dropped for the purposes of agriculture, horticulture or forestry in accordance with the aerial application certificate granted to the operator; also as a measure against weather conditions, surface icing or oil pollution or training for such purposes. When operating in this role, the pilot is exempt from the 500 ft low level flying rule.

The word 'dropping' as used above includes projecting and lowering. Helicopters with a Certificate of Airworthiness endorsement for such duties are exempt from the provisions of this article.

Dropping of persons – Article 44

This has now been separated from dropping articles and animals in the ANO and covers, other than descent of persons by parachute from an aircraft in an emergency:

(i)   Over the UK, a person may not drop, be dropped, permit to be dropped or jump from an aircraft except under and in accordance with the terms of a written permission from CAA. Dropping includes projecting and lowering and must not endanger persons or property.

(ii)   An aircraft must not be used for dropping persons unless express provision is made in the certificate of airworthiness for it.

(iii) Every applicant for and holder of permission must make a parachuting manual available to CAA and this manual must be available to every employee or person engaged in parachuting.

(iv)   The CAA may accept reports from approved persons on dropping of persons from aircraft.

(v)   A person can be lowered in an emergency or for the purpose of saving life.

(vi)   A helicopter can lower a person to the surface if its C of A so permits.

Carriage of weapons and munitions of war – Article 46

Munitions of war means such weapons and ammunition or parts thereof as are designed for use in warfare. It is unlawful to carry, or cause to be carried such articles in an aircraft.

It is now unlawful for a person to carry or have in his charge any weapon while on board any UK registered aircraft. A weapon, not meant for use in warfare, may be carried in an inaccessible part of the aircraft provided that it is not loaded. Weapons may be carried on board an aircraft registered elsewhere than in the UK if such carriage is lawful in the country of registration and they are carried for the safety of the aircraft or the passengers. (This proviso legalises the carriage of so-called security marshals.)

Carriage of dangerous goods – Article 47

(1) Dangerous goods may be carried in an aircraft or underslung as follows:

(i) in accordance with regulations made by the Secretary of State in the case of a variety of dangerous goods:

(ii) with the CAA's permission in writing, and in accordance with any conditions to which such permission may be subject.

(2) The relevant Regulations are the Air Navigation (Dangerous Goods) Regulations and include the following:

(i) 'Dangerous Goods' means any article or substance which a person knows, ought to know or suspects to be goods capable of posing significant risk to health, safety or property when carried by air and which is classified in Part 2 of the Technical Instructions for the Safe Transport of Dangerous Goods by Air approved and published by ICAO, and for which a dangerous goods transport document is required.

(ii) Such dangerous goods may not be transported by air unless the shipper of the goods has (a) prepared in duplicate a dangerous goods transport document and supplied the aircraft operator with a copy and (b) signed a declaration that the Technical Instructions have been complied with, in that the dangerous goods are:

(a) fully and accurately described;

(b) correctly classified, packed, marked and loaded;

(c) in a proper condition for carriage by air.

(iii) The operator must preserve each dangerous goods transport document for 6 months.

(iv) Before dangerous goods are carried, the aircraft operator must carry out an inspection to check:

(a) before accepting the package, that it is marked and labelled in accordance with the Technical Instructions;

(b) that the package is not leaking or damaged so that the contents may escape; also that the unit load device is free from any evidence of leakage.

To carry out this inspection, the operator must use an acceptance check list on which to make his entries, this list to be preserved for six months. If the inspection shows leakage or damage, the package must be unloaded. After dangerous goods are unloaded the operator must inspect the aircraft and equipment and if there has been any contamination or damage, it shall be removed or repaired.

(v) An operator shall not permit an aircraft to fly if it or its equipment has become contaminated by radioactivity.

(vi) The operator is responsible for ensuring dangerous goods are loaded, carried and unloaded in accordance with the provisions of the Technical Instructions. Unless so permitted in the Technical Instructions, dangerous goods may not be carried in the passenger or crew compartments.

(vii) The operator must provide the aircraft commander with the written information specified in the Technical Instructions; the passengers must be informed of the categories of dangerous goods which they cannot take on board as checked or accompanied baggage; the employees must have a CAA-approved training programme as required by the Technical Instructions.

(viii) The operator must, within a reasonable time, produce to an authorised person such of the following documents that may have been requested:

(a) the written permission referred to in (1)(ii) above;

(b) the dangerous goods transport document;

(c) the acceptance check list;

(d) the written information provided to the aircraft commander.

(3) It is unlawful to carry on board, or load on or suspend below an aircraft any goods, the carriage of which is prohibited by this Article.

(4) These rules are in addition to those applicable to the carriage of munitions of war under the previous Article.

(5) Subject to the CAA's written instructions, the Regulations do not apply to any aircraft flying in order to drop articles for the purposes of agriculture, horticulture, forestry, or pollution control.

Method of carriage of persons – Article 48

(i) A person shall only be carried in proper accommodation.

(ii) He will not be towed in anything other than a glider or a flying machine.

(iii) A person may have temporary access to:

(a) any part of the aircraft in the interest of safety;

(b) that part of the aircraft designed to have an access in a cargo plane.

Exits and break-in markings – Article 49

(1) This Article only applies to public transport aircraft registered in the UK.

(2) When carrying passengers, all exits and internal doors are to be kept free of obstructions and not locked during take-off, landing or any emergency unless the exit is not required for use by passengers (and approved by the CAA) or an internal door is so placed as not to prevent or hinder the exit of passengers in an emergency. The flight cabin door is not an exit and may be locked from inside to prevent gunmen and children from entering the flight deck.

(3) Normal exits are to be marked EXIT, whereas emergency exits are to be marked EMERGENCY EXIT (both in CAPITALS).

(4) The above markings must accompany instructions in English and an operating diagram with each exit marking. Where the exits are openable from inside, the markings are placed on or near the inside of the exit; where they are openable from outside, markings are placed on or near the exterior surface.

(5) On aircraft where the maximum total weight authorised is in excess of 3600 kg, 'break-in' areas (areas which are easiest to break from outside in case of emergency) should be marked externally as follows:

(i)   rectangular in shape;

(ii) showing right-angled corners, and

(iii) written in the centre CUT HERE IN EMERGENCY in CAPITALS.

(6) All markings are to be painted in red, but if red is the background colour, or

if red does not contrast with the background colour, then in any contrasting colour.

The term 'maximum total weight authorised' in relation to an aircraft means the maximum total weight of the aircraft and its contents at which the aircraft may take off anywhere in the world, in the most favourable circumstances in accordance with the Certificate of Airworthiness in force in respect of the aircraft.

(7) If one exit (but no more than one) is inoperative and cannot be repaired or replaced at a place, the aircraft may fly to a place where it can be repaired provided that the number of passengers and the positions of the seats they occupy is in accordance with arrangements approved by the Authority. In that case the words 'exit' or 'emergency exit' are covered, and the exit itself marked by a red disc with a horizontal white bar across it bearing the words 'no exit' in red.

Imperilling safety of aircraft – Article 50
A person shall not recklessly or negligently act in a manner likely to endanger an aircraft, or any person therein.

Imperilling safety of any person or property – Article 51
A person shall not recklessly or negligently cause or permit an aircraft to endanger any person or property.

Drunkenness in aircraft – Article 52
(1) A person shall not enter any aircraft when drunk, or be drunk in any aircraft.
(2) As for the crew, the limit of drinking or drug taking is any extent at which capacity to act as a crew member would be impaired.

Smoking in aircraft – Article 53
(1) and (2) Smoking is prohibited when a sign so indicating is displayed in the compartment. In UK registered aircraft, such a sign should be visible from each passenger seat therein.

It is a common misunderstanding of law on this matter that smoking is prohibited during take-off and landing. This is not so; it is prohibited when the sign is displayed.

Authority of commander of aircraft – Article 54
Every person in a UK registered aircraft is to obey all lawful commands of the commander given for the purpose of:
(i) securing the safety of the aircraft and of persons or property carried therein, or
(ii) the safety, efficiency or regularity of air navigation.

*Stowaways – Article 55
A person is not permitted to stowaway.

Exhibitions of flying – Article 56

Persons organising an exhibition of flying at an event which they reasonably believe will be attended by more than 500 persons must first obtain the permission of the Authority unless it is not reasonably foreseeable 7 days before the event that it would be attended by more than 500 persons. The pilot of an aircraft participating in such an exhibition of flying must hold an appropriate display authorisation granted by the Authority. Exhibitions of flying held at aerodromes occupied by the Ministry of Defence or visiting forces will not require permissions, but the Authority may impose conditions on a permission relating to the participation of military aircraft in an exhibition of flying on civilian land.

*Fatigue of crew – application and interpretation – Article 57

(1) The laws here apply to any aircraft registered in the UK which is engaged on a flight for public transport or operated by an air transport undertaking; but they do not apply to flying instruction by or for a flying club or school.

(2) (a) 'flight time' means all the time spent by a crew member in an aircraft registered in the UK or not (other than an aircraft under MTWA 1600 kg not flying for public transport or aerial work) whilst in flight;

(b) 'day' is 24 hours continuous beginning at midnight UTC.

(3) A helicopter is in flight from the first movement under its own power for the purpose of take-off until the rotors are next stopped.

*Fatigue of crew: operator's responsibilities – Article 58

The operator of an aircraft (as specified in Article 57 above) must ensure that flight time limitations are observed and Article 58 specifies that:

(1) An aircraft may not fly unless the operator:

(a) has established a scheme to regulate the flight times of all the crew members, and

(b) the scheme has been approved by CAA;

(c) either the scheme is incorporated in the Operations Manual or a copy is made available to every crew member if no Operations Manual is required;

(d) has taken all practical steps to ensure crew members' compliance with the scheme.

(2) The operator must not allow a crew member to fly if he knows or has reason to believe that the crew member is likely to suffer fatigue and endanger the aircraft and its occupants.

(3) The operator must not allow a crew member to fly unless the operator has an accurate and up to date record for the 28 days immediately preceding the flight for each crew member of:

(a) all flight times;

(b) duties performed in the flight times.

(4) This record (3) must be kept for 12 months after the flight.

Fatigue of crew: responsibility of crew – Article 59

This Article lays down that a person shall not act as a member of crew of any aircraft engaged on a flight for the purpose of public transport or operated by an air transport undertaking in a UK registered aircraft if he believes that he is suffering from, or likely to suffer from, if the flight is undertaken, such fatigue as may endanger the safety of the aircraft or its occupants. A flight crew member must also ensure that the operator of the aircraft is aware of his flight times during the period of 28 days preceding the flight.

Maximum flight times for flight crews – Article 60

(i) Maximum flight time (whether gained in UK registered aircraft or others) is 100 hours in 28 consecutive days expiring at the end of the day on which the flight begins or 900 hours during a period of 12 months expiring at the end of the previous month.

(ii) This rule does not apply to a flight made for purpose *other than* public transport or aerial work:

  (a) in an aircraft not exceeding maximum total weight authorised of 1600 kg, or

  (b) in an aircraft of any weight if the total flight time of the crew member does not exceed 25 hours since last medical. Here, however, there is a further stipulation that the aircraft should not be operated by an air transport undertaking.

    The term 'air transport undertaking' means an undertaking whose business includes the carriage by air of passengers or cargo for hire or reward. The term 'cargo' includes mail and animals.

Documents to be carried – Article 61 and Schedule 11

(1) For aircraft not registered in the UK, the law of the country of registration applies.

(2) For aircraft registered in the UK, if a flight is over the UK only and begins and ends at the same aerodrome, no documents need be carried in the aircraft. Otherwise, the following documents are carried:

  (i) *International flight by public transport aircraft*
    (a) Certificate of Airworthiness;
    (b) Certificate of Registration;
    (c) Certificate of Maintenance Review;
    (d) Radio Licence and Telecommunication Log Book;
    (e) Crew licences;
    (f) One copy of load sheet;
    (g) Technical Log;
    (h) Operations Manual;
    (i) Details of visual signals for aircraft interception and pilot's interception procedures.

    (ii) *Internal flight by public transport aircraft*
       All documents as above, except (b) Certificate of Registration and (i) interception signals and procedures.

   (iii) *International flight: aerial work*
       (a) Certificte of Airworthiness;
       (b) Certificate of Registration;
       (c) Certificate of Maintenance Review;
       (d) Radio Licence and Telecommunication Log Book;
       (e) Crew Licences;
       (f) Technical Log;
       (g) Details of visual signals for aircraft interception and pilot's interception procedures.

   (iv) *Internal flight: aerial work*
       All documents applicable to (iii) above, except (b) Certificate of Registration and (g) interception signals and procedures.

    (v) *International flight: private flight*
       (a) Certificate of Airworthiness;
       (b) Certificate of Registration;
       (c) Radio Licence and Telecommunication Log Book;
       (d) Crew Licences.

Note that under Article 26, the Operations Manual need not be carried if the aircraft is being used solely for training flights or it begins and ends at the same aerodrome and the duration of the flight does not exceed one hour. Also, with CAA's permission, the flight manual need not be carried as part of the C of A when an operations manual is carried provided that the Operations Manual contains data from the flight manual on Limitations and Emergency Procedures together with performance instructions.

    For the purpose of this Article, flight to the Channel Islands, the Isle of Man and any country to which there is power to extend the Act, or any British Protected State, is not an international flight.

Production of documents and records – Article 63
(1) *Within reasonable time*
    (a) The commander of the aircraft must produce all documents required to be carried under Article 61 and Schedule 11 and Certificate of Registration, Certificate of Airworthiness and Crew Licences on being requested to do so within reasonable time. The term 'reasonable time' is not defined and its interpretation depends on relevant circumstances.
    (b) An individual should produce his personal flying log book after being requested to do so within reasonable time, to an authorised person.
(3) *Within 5 days*
    A holder of a licence shall produce his licence, including any certificate of

validation and any medical certificate, to an authorised person within 5 days, if that licence was not required to be carried in the aircraft.

(4) *Within 2 years*
Every person who is required to keep a log book must be prepared to produce it up to 2 years after the date of the last entry therein.

Offences in relation to documents and records – Article 68

(1) A person shall not with intent to deceive:
  (i) *use* any licence, certificate, approval, permission, exemption or other document which has been forged, altered, revoked, suspended or to which he is not entitled;
  (ii) *lend* any licence, certificate, approval, exemption, etc., to any other person, or
  (iii) *procure* any licence, etc., for himself or any other person by false representation.
  Any reference in this paragraph to licence, approval, etc., includes a copy or purported copy thereof.
(2) A person shall not mutilate, alter or render illegible any log book or other document required under this order, or help any other to do so, or make a false entry or commit a material omission, or destroy any such document.
(3) All entries in a log book or record are to be in ink or indelible pencil.
(4) A person shall not knowingly make in a load sheet an incorrect entry in a material particular, or any material omission.

The Rules of the Air Regulations – Article 69

The Rules of the Air Regulations published as a separate Statutory Instrument, are binding, with one minor exception, on:
  (a) all aircraft within the United Kingdom; and
  (b) all aircraft registered in the United Kingdom, wherever they may be.
(2) It is an offence to contravene, to permit the contravention of, or to fail to comply with the Rules of the Air except:
(3) (i) when avoiding immediate danger, or
  (ii) when complying with the law of the country the aircraft is in, or
  (iii) when complying with Military Flying Regulations or Flying Orders issued by the Secretary of State in relation to an aircraft of which the commander is acting as such in the course of his duty as a member of H.M. Forces.
(4) If the contravention was made to avoid immediate danger, the pilot must report the matter within 10 days of the incident as follows:
  (a) to the competent authority of the country in whose territory the incident occurred;
  (b) to the CAA if it occurred over the high seas.
(5) No provision in the Rules of Air exonerates a person from the consequences of:
  (i) neglect in the use of lights or signals;
  (ii) neglect of normal precautions, in all circumstances.

Power to prohibit or restrict flying – Article 74

(1) The Secretary of State may restrict or prohibit flying over certain areas in the following circumstances:
   (i)   when there is a large gathering of people;
   (ii) in the vicinity of an aircraft race, exhibition of flying or contest;
   (iii) for reasons of national defence or reasons affecting public interests.
   The prohibition may apply generally to all aircraft, or to particular types or class.

(2) If an aircraft contravenes the prohibition under (1)(iii) above, (i.e. danger area) the commander shall take the following action:
   (i)   not commence descent while over such area;
   (ii) leave the area by the shortest route;
   (iii) comply with any instructions issued by the controlling authority.

Successive Pink Information Circulars have been issued invoking this Order in the event of a disaster occurring on land or at sea within the UK FIR. Any disaster, particularly those involving gas, or chemical installations with a risk of explosion, fire and surface pollution, release of noxious gases, will bring in the Emergency Controlling Authority (ECA) from one of the various agencies: the ECA may wish to inhibit flying in the vicinity of the disaster by aircraft not directly engaged with emergency action, and the reasons for this are clear. If a temporary Danger Area fails to achieve the objective (where, for example, the disaster has aroused a great deal of public interest), ANO Article 74 will be invoked and published in a NOTAM Class 1: thus, it will be an offence to fly in the designated area without permission, and only the ECA (which will be identified) can give permission. En route traffic, company aircraft, the press and television will be well down the priority list.

Pilots airborne in the vicinity of a disaster should move upwind of the area as quickly as possible and assume that airspace restrictions have been imposed. And, of course, a pilot will report to any ATS unit at once if he sees a disaster which has not, to his knowledge, been notified.

Balloons, kites, airships, gliders, parascending parachutes – Article 75

Within the UK, without the permission of the CAA (in writing) and subject to any conditions laid down by CAA:

(a) a captive balloon or kite cannot be flown at a height of more than 60 m above ground level or within 60 m of any vessel, vehicle or structure;
(b) a captive balloon cannot be flown within 5 km of an aerodrome;
(c) a balloon exceeding 2 m in any linear dimension at any stage of its flight, including any basket or other equipment attached to the balloon, cannot be flown in controlled airspace notified for the purpose of this Article.
(d) a kite shall not be flown within 5 km of an aerodrome;
(e) an airship shall not be moored;
(f) a glider or parascending parachute may not be launched by winch and cable or by ground tow to a height of more than 60 m above ground level.

Also, a captive balloon when in flight must be securely moored and not left unattended unless it is fitted with a device which ensures its automatic deflation if it breaks free of its moorings.

Aerodromes: public transport of passengers and instruction in flying – Article 76

(1) For the aircraft covered by this Article, take-offs and landings are only permitted at either:
    (i) a Government aerodrome or a CAA owned or managed aerodrome which is notified as available for such take-off and landing, or where permission has been obtained; or
    (ii) an aerodrome licensed for the purpose.

(2) This Article applies to:
    (a) aeroplanes of MTWA exceeding 2730 kg and flying for the purpose of:
        (i) public transport of passengers; or
        (ii) flying instruction to qualify for a licence or rating;
        (iii) flight tests of persons qualifying for a licence or rating.
    (b) aeroplanes of MTWA not exceeding 2730 kg engaged on:
        (i) scheduled journeys for public transport of passengers;
        (ii) public transport of passengers on flights beginning and ending at the same aerodrome;
        (iii) as (2)(a)(ii) and (2)(a)(iii) above;
        (iv) public transport of passengers on night flights;
    (c) Helicopters and gyroplanes as (2)(b)(i) and (2)(b)(iii) above
    (d) And lastly, it applies to gliders which are flying for the purpose of the public transport of passengers or for the purpose of instruction in flying. It does not apply to gliders being flown under arrangements made by a flying club and carrying no person other than a member of the club.

(3) A helicopter engaged at night for the purpose of the public transport of passengers shall ensure that if it intends to take off or land at a place other than the place specified in para (1) above, the person in charge of the area has caused such lighting to be in operation that the pilot may make a safe take-off and, in the case of landing, be able to identify the landing area in flight, to determine the landing direction and make a safe approach and landing.

Aviation fuel at aerodromes – Article 87

(3) A person shall not cause or permit any aviation fuel to be dispensed for use in an aircraft if he knows or has reason to believe that the aviation fuel is not fit for use in aircraft. If it appears that unfit fuel is likely to be dispensed, the CAA or an authorised person may direct the person having the management of the installation not to permit aviation fuel to be dispensed until the direction has been revoked by the CAA or the authorised person.

(4) 'Aviation fuel' means fuel intended for use in aircraft and 'aviation fuel installation' means any apparatus or container, including a vehicle, designed, manufactured or adapted for the storage of aviation fuel or for the delivery of such fuel to an aircraft.

*Mandatory reporting – Article 94 and air navigation regulation 17
This is allied with the Air Navigation (General) Regulations and specified for
your study. Reportable occurrences are listed there at Regulation 17; those:

(a) involving damage to the aircraft;
(b) involving injury to a person;
(c) involving the impairment during flight of a crew member's capacity to
     continue his duties;
(d) involving the use in flight of any procedures to overcome an emergency;
(e) involving the failure of an aircraft system or of any aircraft equipment;
(f) arising from the control of an aircraft in flight by its flight crew;
(g) arising from failure or inadequacy of ground facilities or services intended to
     be used in an aircraft's operation;
(h) arising from the loading or carrying of passengers, cargo (including mail),
     fuel, from anything not referred to above, and any other occurrence which,
     in the opinion of the persons listed in Article 94 (as follows) would endanger,
     if not corrected, the safety of an aircraft, its occupants or any other person.

The report shall contain the following information:

(a) type, series and registration marks of the aircraft;
(b) name of operator;
(c) date of the reportable occurrence;
(d) if the person making the report has started an investigation, and, if so, has
     it been completed or not;
(e) details and effects of the occurrence;
(f) if in flight:
     (i)   GMT of the occurrence;
     (ii)   last point of departure and intended destination at that time;
     (iii) aircraft's geographical position at that time.
(g) if it is a defect of an aircraft or any part or equipment, the name of the
     manufacturer, its part number and location on the aircraft;
(h) signature, name in block letters of the person making the report, his
     employer, and the capacity in which he acts for that employer;
(i) if made by the Commander, Engineer, or Air Traffic Controller, a contact
     address and phone number must be given, if ready contact at his place of
     employment is unavailable.

The following may report:

(a) the commander of a public transport aircraft, registered in the UK and
     having a maximum weight authorised of more than 2300 kg;
(b) an aircraft manufacturer, or one who carries on a business of repairing or
     overhauling such an aircraft or its equipment;
(c) an engineer who signs a certificate of maintenance review, or release to
     service in respect of such aircraft or its equipment;

(d) a licensed Air Traffic Controller;

(e) a licensee or manager of a licensed aerodrome.

The report is made to the Authority within 96 hours. Any flight data recorder relevant to the reportable occurrence must be preserved for fourteen days from the date of the report, or any such longer period as the Authority may direct. However, in case the aircraft is outside the UK and it is not reasonably practicable to preserve the record until the aircraft returns to the UK, the record may be erased.

Penalties – Article 99

Subject to provisos that allow an operator or aircraft commander to prove that he was unaware of any contrvention of the ANO or of any Regulations made under the ANO, any person who contravenes any provision of the ANO or any Regulations made under the ANO, will be liable on conviction to a fine not exceeding £400. However, for a contravention of any provision under some fifty-odd articles (or sub-articles) ranging from not keeping log books, pilots not remaining at controls, flight time limitations to breach of the Rules of the Air, the fine on summary conviction can be up to £1000. For contravention of the articles listed in Part B of schedule 12 (which range from endangering safety, drunks in aircraft, flying when in a dangerous state of fatigue to making false reports) on summary conviction the penalty is a fine not exceeding £2000 and on conviction on indictment to a fine or imprisonment for a term not exceeding two years or both.

Interpretation – Article 106

You should be familiar with the following further definitions:

Aerial work means any purpose (other than public transport) for which an aircraft is flown if valuable consideration is given, or promised, in respect of the flight or the purpose of the flight.

With effect from 1 April 1989 this definition was substantially revised by the addition of Article 107 to the ANO. For example, the following are not deemed to be aerial work but are treated as private flights:

(1) a flight for the purpose of taking part in an aircraft race, contest or exhibition of flying notwithstanding the payment to the owner or operator of the actual costs of the flight or the award to the pilot of a prize which does not exceed a specified limit;

(2) a flight in respect of which the only payment is made to a registered charity and which is carried out with the written permission of the CAA;

(3) a flight on which no more than four persons are carried and who each bear a proportionate share of the actual costs of the flight;

(4) a flight in respect of which the pilot reclaims the actual costs from his employer;

(5) a flight in an aircraft which is jointly owned when the only payment in

respect of the flight reflects its actual costs and is paid by one or more of the joint owners.

However, a flight in which 'valuable consideration' has been given or promised for the carriage of passengers, which flight is for the purpose of dropping persons by parachute and which is carried out in accordance with the CAA's written permission *is* an aerial work flight. Similarly, a positioning flight made prior to such a parachute dropping flight and the return of the aircraft to its base after such a parachute dropping flight are also aerial work flights.

Aerodrome means any area of land or water, designed, equipped, set apart or commonly used for affording facilities for the take-off and landing of aircraft (not being an area abandoned for those purposes).

Aeronautical radio station means a radio station on the surface, which transmits or receives signals for the purpose of assisting aircraft.

Aerodrome traffic zone means:

(a) except for an offshore installation (i) at an aerodrome at which the longest runway is notified as 1850 m or less, the airspace from the surface to 2000 ft above the aerodrome level, and within the area bounded by a circle of 2 nm radius centred on the notified mid-point of the longest runway, (ii) at an aerodrome at which the longest runway is notified as greater than 1850 m, the air space from the surface to 2000 ft above aerodrome level within the area bounded by a circle of 2.5 nm radius centred on the notified mid-point of the longest runway;

    This would also apply to any aerodrome in (a)(i) above if the ATZ would otherwise extend less than 1.5 nm beyond the end of the runway.

(b) in the case of an offshore installation, ditto, but 2000 ft above msl and within $1\frac{1}{2}$ nm of the installation.

Unless, of course, part of the airspace is within the zone of another aerodrome notified as the controlling aerodrome.

Authorised person means:

(a) any constable, and

(b) any person authorised by the CAA or Secretary of State, either generally, or in relation to a particular case or class of cases.

Competent authority means, in relation to the UK, the CAA; and in relation to any other country, means the authority responsible under the law of that country for promoting the safety of civil aviation.

Crew means members of the flight crew, persons carried for the purpose of testing or inspecting flight crew and cabin attendants.

Cross country flight means any flight during the course of which the aircraft is more than 3 nm from the aerodrome of departure.

Flight level means one of a series of levels of equal atmospheric pressure, separated by notified intervals, and each expressed as the number of hundreds of feet which would be indicated at that level on a pressure altimeter calibrated in accordance with the ISA and set to 1013.2 mb.

Licence – definition. Licence includes any certificate of competency or certificate of validity issued with the licence or required to be held in connection with the licence by the law of the country in which the licence is granted.

Life jacket includes any device designed to support a person individually in or on the water.

Microlight aeroplane means an aeroplane having a maximum total weight authorised (MTWA) not exceeding 390 kg, a wing loading at MTWA not exceeding 25 kg per square metre, a maximum fuel capacity not exceeding 50 litres and which has been designed to carry not more than 2 persons.

Night means the time between half an hour after sunset and half an hour before sunrise (both times inclusive), sunset and sunrise being determined at surface level.

Nautical mile means the International Nautical Mile, that is to say 1852 m.

Parascending parachute means a parachute towed by a cable so it is caused to ascend.

Passenger, when the term is used in the ANO, means any person other than a member of the crew.

Private flight means a flight which is neither for aerial work nor for public transport.

Public transport aircraft means an aircraft flying, or intended by the operator of the aircraft to fly, for the purpose of public transport if valuable consideration is given or promised for the carriage of passengers or cargo in the aircraft on that flight. (It includes (a) the gratuitous carriage by the air transport undertaking of cargo or passengers not employed by the undertaking and (b) when valuable consideration is given or promised primarily for a particular person to have the right to fly the aircraft on that flight providing it is not a single seat aircraft of 910 kg or less maximum weight authorised.) Again, Article 107 moves certain flights to private flights as already described under *Aerial work*.

Scheduled journey means one of a series of journeys which are undertaken between the same two places and which together amount to a systematic service.

Solo flight means a flight on which the pilot of the aircraft is not accompanied by a person holding a valid pilot's licence.

In addition to the schedules 3, 4, 8 and 11 already mentioned on the foregoing pages, pilots are also to know the contents of:

Schedule 1A – the general classification of aircraft;

Schedule 2   – the 'A' and 'B' conditions under which an aircraft can be given special conditions to fly and their limitations;

Schedule 5   – the radio equipment required to be carried in an aircraft. Although the table looks formidable at first glance, in fact the scales of equipment show a steady increase as the complexity of the flight conditions increases, and can soon be rationalised.

It should be noted that although most definitions of aeronautical terms are given in Article 106, schedule 5 contains radio equipment definitions.

17
Rules of the Air, Display of Lights by Aircraft, Marshalling Signals

Rules of the air

The following rules for avoiding collisions, both in the air and on the ground, are prescribed in the Rules of the Air Regulations, with the proviso that, notwithstanding that the flight is being made with air traffic control clearance, it shall remain the duty of the commander of an aircraft to take all possible measures to ensure that his aircraft does not collide with any other aircraft.

(1) An aircraft is prohibited from flying in such proximity to other aircraft as to create a danger of collision.

(2) An aircraft is not permitted to formate with other aircraft unless the commanders have agreed to do so.

(3) For the purposes of this rule, a glider and a flying machine which is towing it is considered to be a single aircraft, under the command of the commander of the towing flying machine.

(4) Under the following rules one aircraft may have a right of way; the other may be obliged to give way. The one who has right of way shall maintain its heading and speed. The one who is obliged to give way shall avoid passing over or under the other aircraft, or crossing ahead of it, unless passing well clear of it.

Rules of right of way in flight

Two aircraft in flight

(a) *Two aircraft converging.* Where the aircraft are converging and one must give way to the other, if the aircraft are of different class, the rule of precedence applies. The order of precedence is as follows:

First   – Balloons
Second – Gliders
Third   – Airships
Last   – Flying machines

Where two aircraft are of the same class (e.g. two flying machines), the rule is that the aircraft which has the other on its right shall give way, except that mechanically driven aircraft shall give way to aircraft towing other aircraft or objects. (See Fig. 17.1.)

(b) *Two aircraft approaching head-on.* Each alters heading to its right.

(c) *Overtaking.* An aircraft which is being overtaken in the air has the right of way. An overtaking aircraft, whether climbing, descending or in level flight, has the duty to keep out of the way of the other aircraft by altering

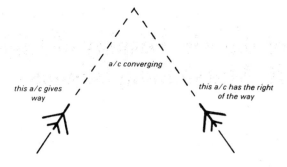

Fig. 17.1

its heading to the right. It will continue to keep clear of the other aircraft until that other aircraft has been passed and is clear, notwithstanding any change in the relative positions of the two.

A glider overtaking another glider, in the UK, may alter its heading right or left.

(d) *Landing and take-off.* Already referred to in Chapter 8, Flight at Aerodromes, the following rules also apply. Where take-offs and landings are not confined to a runway then:

(1) an aircraft taking off must leave on its left any aircraft which has already taken off or is about to take off;

(2) an aircraft landing must leave on its left any aircraft which has landed, is already landing or is about to take off, and subsequently turn left;

(3) an aircraft after landing must move clear of the landing area as soon as possible unless instructed otherwise;

(4) take-offs and landings should be in the direction indicated by ground signals or if there are no such signals, into wind, unless good aviation practice requires otherwise.

Rules of right of way on the ground

An aircraft shall not taxi on the apron or manoeuvring area of an aerodrome without permission, as appropriate, from either the ATC unit or the person in charge of the aerodrome.

(a) Between aircraft and vehicles the rules of precedence are these:

First   – Taking off and landing aircraft
Second – Vehicles towing aircraft
Third   – Aircraft
Last   – Vehicles

(b) Subject to the above

(i) when two flying machines on the ground are approaching head on, each shall alter its heading to the right;

(ii) when two flying machines are on converging courses, the one which has the other on its right shall give way and shall avoid crossing ahead of the other unless passing well clear of it;

(iii) a flying machine which is being overtaken has the right of way, and the overtaking flying machine shall keep out of the way of the other flying machine by altering its heading to the *left* until that other flying machine has been passed and is clear, notwithstanding any change in the relative positions of the two flying machines.

(5) Right-hand traffic rule
An aircraft flying in the UK within sight of the ground and following a road, railway, or other similar landmark, is to keep such landmark on its left.

(6) Aerobatic manoeuvres
Such manoeuvres are not permitted over the congested area of any city, town or settlement or within controlled airspace. In the case of controlled airspace, such manoeuvres may be carried out with the permission of the appropriate ATC unit.

**(7) Simulated instrument flight*
An aircraft is not permitted to fly in simulated instrument flight conditions unless:
(a) the aircraft is fitted with serviceable dual controls, and
(b) a safety pilot is carried in the second control seat who can render assistance to the pilot flying the aircraft if necessary, and
(c) if the safety pilot's field of vision is not adequate, both forward and to each side, a third person who is a competent observer is also carried. He should occupy a position from which he can make good the deficiency in the field of vision of the safety pilot and he should be in direct communication with him.

**(8) Practice instrument approaches*
Within the UK, practice instrument approaches may only be carried out in VMC on the following conditions:
(a) the appropriate air traffic control unit should be informed in advance;
(b) and if the instrument conditions are not being simulated, then a competent observer should be carried. He should be placed in a position giving an adequate field of vision and should be able to communicate readily with the pilot flying the aircraft.

Display of lights by aircraft
Flying machines of any country while in, or flying over the UK at night are required to comply with the following rules for the display of lights. If an aircraft has an anti-collision light it must also display it by day.
(1)(a) Flying machines stationary on the apron or maintenance area – no lights are required to be displayed, except for a red anti-collision light if fitted, if engine(s) are running by day or night.
  (b) Flying machines moving on any part of the aerodrome:
    (i) all lights on which would be on if in flight, or

(ii) three basic lights, steady or flashing.

The *basic lights* are:

(1) A *green light* of at least five candela showing to the starboard side through an angle of 110° from dead ahead in the horizontal plane.

(2) A *red light* of at least five candela showing to the port side through an angle of 110° from dead ahead in the horizontal plane.

(3) A *white light* of at least three candela showing through angles of 70° from dead astern to each side in the horizontal plane.

(c) Flying machines registered in the UK having a maximum total weight authorised of more than 5700 kg or any other flying machine registered in the UK after April 1988 must display:

(i) basic lights, steady and

(ii) anti-collision light.

Anti-collision light in respect of rotorcraft means a flashing red light showing in all directions for the purpose of enabling the aircraft to be more readily detected by the pilots of distant aircraft. In respect of all other aircraft, it may be either a flashing red light or a flashing white light.

(d) Flying machines registered in the UK before 1 April 1988 having a maximum total weight authorised of 5700 kg and below must display:

(i) three basic lights – all steady, or

(ii) three basic lights, steady, and an anti-collision light, or

(iii) three basic lights flashing. In this case, it is mandatory that an additional light, white in colour, of at least 20 candela and showing in all directions, be installed and that the three basic lights flash in alternation with the white light which is also flashing. An anti-collision light may be added at option.

(e) Any other flying machine must display:

(i) three basic lights, steady, or

(ii) three basic lights, steady, plus anti-collision light, or

(iii) three basic lights, flashing with or without anti-collision light, or

(iv) three basic lights flashing in alternation with white as described above, with or without anti-collision light, or

(v) three basic lights, flashing in alternation with a red light, at least 20 candela, installed in the tail and showing through same angles as the white tail light, and with or without anti-collision light, or

(vi) three basic lights, flashing in alternation with both white and red lights, with or without anti-collision light.

(2) If by reason of the physical construction of the aircraft it is necessary to fit more than one lamp in order to show the required light, the lamps should be so fitted that, so far as is reasonably practicable, not more than one such lamp is visible from any one point outside the aircraft.

(3) Where the lights are to be shown through specific angles in the horizontal plane, they should also be visible through 90° above and below in the vertical plane. This means that the same light which is visible to an aircraft, say, approaching from the rear, is also visible to it above or below the aircraft.

(4) In the UK, if a navigation light fails in flight and cannot be immediately replaced or repaired, the aircraft should land as soon as it can safely do so

unless the appropriate air traffic control unit authorises continuance of the flight. If the light fails while taxiing out, the aircraft must not take-off until the light has been replaced or repaired.
(Note: the use of the term 'basic lights' above is the author's expression for simplicity of explanation and not an authorised term.)

(5) A helicopter stationary on an off-shore installation is allowed (in accordance with its Operations Manual procedure) to switch off its anti-collision light as a signal to ground personnel that it is safe to approach the helicopter to embark/disembark passengers and/or load or unload cargo.

(6) *Lights on captive balloons and kites*
The following rules apply when flying at night at a height exceeding 60 m:
(a) A group of two steady lights is installed, consisting of a white light placed 4 m above a red light, both being of at least five candela and showing in all directions, the white light being placed not less than 5 m and not more than 10 m below the basket or the lowest part of the balloon.
(b) The above group is to be repeated along the mooring cable every 300 m interval, the lowest group to be shown below the cloud base.
(c) On the surface, a group of three flashing lights, forming approximately an equilateral triangle is installed. The sides of the triangle are approximately 25 m and the triangle is so arranged that the horizontal projection of the mooring cable occurs along one of the sides at 90°, and this side is marked by two red lights (the remaining light of the triangle being green). The triangle encloses the object on the surface to which the balloon or kite is moored.

It should be borne in mind that a captive balloon or kite has its mooring cable marked during daylight hours too if flying more than 60 m above the surface. Tubular streamers must be attached to the cable at intervals of not more than 200 m measured from the lowest part of the basket, or if there is no basket, from the lowest part of the balloon. The streamers have alternate 50 cm wide bands of red and white with overall dimensions of at least 2 m long and 40 cm diameter. For a kite, alternatively the cable can have at intervals of 100 m from the lowest point of the kite, streamers not less than 80 cm long and 30 cm wide at their widest, marked with alternate bands of red and white 10 cm wide.

(7) *Free balloons*
A free balloon at night shall display a steady red light, at least 5 candela showing in all directions, suspended not less than 5 m and not more than 10 m below the basket or below the lowest part of the balloon, if there is no basket.

(8) *Gliders*
A glider while flying at night may display any system of lights pertaining to an aircraft or simply a steady red light of at least 5 candela showing in all directions.

(9) *Airships*
In flight, the rules are similar to those for flying machines but there are additional lights for the control car when the engines are stopped.

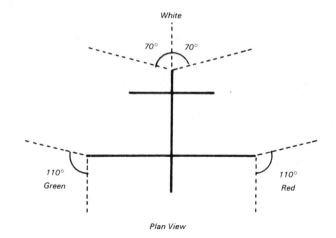

Plan View

Fig. 17.2

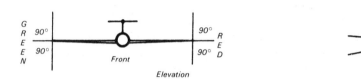

Fig. 17.3

(10) *Flying machines – diagram in plan and elevation*

(11) *Avoiding collisions*

When a light of another aircraft is seen at night and appears to be at one's own level, the risk of a collision may exist. A very simple rule resolves the possibility, or otherwise, of a collision. The rule is: estimate the relative bearing of the visible light of the aircraft at short intervals; *if the relative bearings remain fairly constant throughout, a risk of collision exists* and appropriate action to avoid collision *must be taken* in good time. What action you take will depend on whether you have the right of way, or are obliged to give way. It should, however, be borne in mind that even though you have right of way, if the other aircraft does not give way, it is your responsibility to do all that is possible to avoid collision.

Alternatively, if it is found that the relative bearing of the other aircraft does not remain constant – it either increases or decreases – there is no risk of collision. Just keep an eye on the other aircraft until it is a safe distance away.

(12) *To determine the possible limits of heading of another aircraft*

Simply by sighting one light of an aircraft, that aircraft's possible limits of its headings can be estimated quickly. (See Fig. 17.4.)

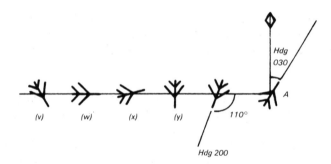

Fig. 17.4

If the pilot of aircraft A, steering 030°(T) sights another aircraft on a relative bearing of 240° in position (v), it can be appreciated from the diagram that its red light would be visible. However, if that aircraft was steering heading (w), you would *just* see his red light (along with green), since you are now looking at the aircraft along its centreline. A slight alteration of the heading to that shown in position x will change the light, and you would see its green light. Therefore, the heading shown in position (w) is one limit of his heading when it is possible to see the red light. It is apparent that this heading is 090°(T) from the diagram. Arithmetically, this is worked out as follows:

A's True Heading	030	
Add relative bearing	240	
True bearing	270	
Add or subtract	180	*first limit*
	090	

As for the second limit of the heading, as we have seen in Fig. 17.4, if the observed aircraft altered its heading even slightly from 090° to north, its green light would become visible (x). But, if it altered further south, say to position (y), the red light would still be visible, since we know that the red light is visible through an angle of 110° from the aircraft's dead ahead. In this case, therefore, as long as the aircraft is steering a heading of 090° + 110° = 200°, its red light will remain visible. This is the *second limit* of its heading. Any further alteration of the heading in the same direction, say, 201°, will make its tail light visible. Therefore, if aircraft A sights another aircraft on a relative bearing of 240°, and sees its red light, that other aircraft must be steering a heading between 090° and 200°. On the same principle, limits may be calculated when the green light is seen. The rules of estimation are summarised below.

When a red or green navigation light is sighted:

(a) Add your own true heading to the estimated relative bearing of the other aircraft. This gives the true bearing of the other aircraft.
(b) If this true bearing comes to a figure above 360°, subtract 360° from it at this stage.

(c) Add or subtract as necessary 180° and the answer is the first limit.
(d) If the light sighted is red, add 110° to the first limit to obtain the second limit. If the light sighted is green, subtract 110° from the first limit to get the second limit.
(e) Always designate your answer by a quadrantal or cardinal point through which the change of one limit to another takes place. For example, in the above illustration, the answer would be 090° to 200° through South.

In the following diagram, Fig. 17.5, aircraft A, again doing 030(T), sights another aircraft on a relative bearing of 240° but, in this instance, it sights its white tail light. From the diagram we see that the other aircraft's heading is 270°(T), and that aircraft A is sighting that aircraft from dead astern. We also know from the law that if that aircraft altered its heading through 70° either side of 270°, as shown in position (y) and (z), we should still see the white light, but those headings will be the limits. Any further alteration of heading in a northerly or southerly direction will result in the change over of the light to green or red.

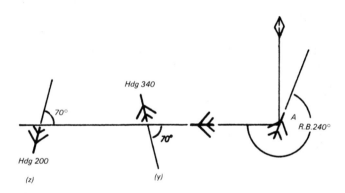

Hdg 340

70°

70°

A
R.B.240°

Hdg 200

(z)

(y)

Fig. 17.5

Based on this reasoning, the rule of estimation of limits of headings, when a tail light is sighted is, as follows:
(a) Add your own true heading to the estimated relative bearing of the other aircraft and find its true bearing, as before.
(b) Add *and* subtract 70° to the true bearing. This gives the two limits. In the above illustration (Fig. 17.5):

A's True heading   030
Relative bearing   <u>240</u>
True bearing   270

True bearing	270		True bearing	270
Add	<u>070</u>		Subtract	<u>070</u>
	340 – *one limit*			200 – *other limit*

These values of course check up with the previously determined limits of the other aircraft's green and red navigation lights.

It is in the Rules of the Air Regulations that the definitions of anti-collision light, apron, hang glider and manoeuvring area are given, among others:

Anti-collision light means:

(a) in relation to a rotorcraft a flashing red light;

(b) in relation to any other aircraft a flashing red or a flashing white light;

and in either case showing in all directions so as to allow the aircraft to be more readily seen by pilots from distance.

Apron means the part of an aerodrome provided for the stationing of aircraft for the embarkation and disembarkation of passengers, the loading and unloading of cargo and for parking.

Hang glider means any glider capable of being:

(a) carried, (b) foot-launched and (c) landed solely by the energy and use of the pilot's legs.

Manoeuvring area means the part of an aerodrome provided for the take-off and landing of aircraft and the movement of aircraft on the surface, excluding the apron and the aircraft maintenance area.

Marshalling signals

(a) Marshaller to pilot

The following are the signals made by a marshaller to assist the ground manoeuvres of aircraft. It is, however, emphasised that the ultimate responsibility of avoiding a taxiing incident rests with the pilot. The pilot may, therefore, ignore the signals if he considers it unwise to comply with them. The most common signals are shown below.

Meaning of signal	Description of signal
(1) Proceed under guidance of another marshaller	Right or left arm down, the other arm moved across body and extended to indicate position of the other marshaller. (Fig. 17.6.)
(2) Move ahead	Arms repeatedly moved upward and backward, beckoning onward. (Fig. 17.7.)
(3) Open up starboard engine or turn to port	Right arm down, left arm repeatedly moved upward and backward. The speed of arm movement indicates the rate of turn. (Fig. 17.8.)
(4) Open up port engine or turn to starboard	Left arm down, the right arm repeatedly moved upward and backward. The speed of arm movement indicates the rate of turn. (Fig. 17.9.)
(5) Stop	Arms repeatedly crossed above the head. The speed of arm movement indicates the urgency of the stop. (Fig. 17.10.)
(6) Start engines	A circular motion of the right hand at head level, with the left arm pointing to the appropriate engine. (Fig. 17.11.)

(7) Chocks inserted	Arms extended, the palms facing inwards, then swung from the extended position inwards. (Fig. 17.12.)
(8) Chocks away	Arms down, the palms facing outwards, then swung outwards. (Fig. 17.13.)
(9) Cut engines	Either arm and hand placed level with the chest, then moved laterally with the palm downwards. (Fig. 17.14.)
(10) Slow down	Arms placed down, with the palms towards the ground, then moved up and down several times. (Fig. 17.15.)
(11) Slow down engines on indicated side	Arms placed down, with the palms towards the ground, then either the right or left arm moved up and down indicating that the motors on the left or right side, as the case may be, should be slowed down. (See Fig. 17.16.)
(12) This bay	Arms placed above the head in a vertical position. (See Fig. 17.17.)
(13) All clear: marshalling finished	The right arm raised at the elbow, with the arm facing forward. (See Fig. 17.18.)

Other marshalling signals relate to 'push backs', engaging and releasing breakes, helicopter movements, releasing loads, etc. and in the UK are listed in the Rules of the Air Regulations.

(b) Pilot to Marshaller

Meaning of signal	Description of signal
(1) Brakes applied	Arm and hand with fingers extended in front of face, then clench fist.
(2) Brakes released	Fist clenched in front of face, then extend fingers.
(3) Insert chocks	Arms extended, palms outwards, then move hands inwards to cross in front of face.
(4) Remove chocks	Hands crossed in front of face, palms outwards, then move arms outwards.
(5) Ready to start engine(s)	Raise number of fingers on one hand to indicate the engine (Port outer = 1 etc.).

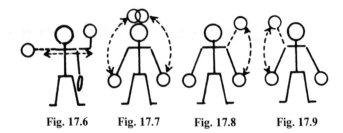

Fig. 17.6   Fig. 17.7   Fig. 17.8   Fig. 17.9

Fig. 17.10   Fig. 17.11

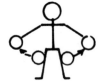

Fig. 17.12   Fig. 17.13   Fig. 17.14

Fig. 17.15   Fig. 17.16   Fig. 17.17   Fig. 17.18

18
Security, Interceptions and Accidents

Reference was made in Chapter 1 to Annex 17 and to the Tokyo Convention, which are concerned with matters of security. The following terms have specific definitions in this connection, not covered in earlier chapters.

Airside The movement area of an airport, adjacent terrain and buildings or portions thereof, access to which is controlled.

Security A combination of measures and human and material resources intended to safeguard international civil aviation against acts of unlawful interference.

Security control A means by which the introduction of weapons, explosives or articles likely to be utilised to commit an act of unlawful interference can be prevented.

Security programme Measures adopted to safeguard international civil aviation against acts of unlawful interference.

General objective

It is ICAO's general objective that every contracting state shall establish measures to prevent weapons, explosives or any other dangerous devices which may be used to commit an act of unlawful interference, the carriage or bearing of which is not authorised, from being introduced, by any means whatsoever, on board an aircraft engaged in international civil aviation. In particular, special attention must be paid to the threat posed by explosive devices concealed in, or using electric, electronic or battery-operated items carried as hand-baggage and/ or in checked baggage. There is an ICAO security manual (Document 8973) which gives guidance on this latter topic.

Organisation

(1) Nationally, each contracting state is recommended to ensure that arrangements are made for the inspection of suspected sabotage devices or other potential hazards at airports serving international civil aviation and for their disposal. Also, each contracting state should promote whenever possible, research and development of new security equipment which will better satisfy international civil aviation security objectives.

(2) Internationally, it is recommended that contracting states should also co-operate with other states in the field of research and development on security equipment and when any state makes a bilateral agreement on air transport, a clause in that treaty should relate to aviation security.

(3) Some states allow their airline(s) to carry what are usually known as 'Sky Marshalls'. A number of ICAO recommendations relate to this practice, such as:

(a) Contracting states should ensure that carriage of weapons on board aircraft by law enforcement officers etc. must have special authorisations in accordance with the laws of the state(s) concerned.

(b) In other cases, an authorised person must check that any weapons carried are not loaded and the weapons are stowed in a place which is inaccessible during flight.

(c) Contracting states must ensure that the pilot knows the number of armed persons on board the aircraft and where they are seated.

Routine procedures

Routine procedures which are recommended by ICAO for contracting states are:

(1) Ensure that pre-flight checks of aircraft assigned to international flights include measures to discover weapons, explosives and sabotage or other dangerous devices which may have been placed on board.

(2) Require operators providing service from that state, to include in their security programmes, measures and procedures to ensure safety on board their aircraft when passengers are to be carried who are obliged to travel because they have been the subject of judicial or administrative proceedings.

(3) Require measures to be taken to ensure that disembarking passengers do not leave items on board aircraft.

Baggage

Unaccompanied baggage is always a potential security problem and ICAO has addressed this problem by recommending contracting states:

(1) To ensure that operators when providing a service from that state do not transport the baggage of passengers who are not on board the aircraft unless the baggage separated from the passenger is subjected to other security control measures.

(2) To establish measures to ensure that consignments of packages and checked baggage intended for carriage on passenger flights and using commercial courier services, are also subjected to specific security control, additional to (1) above.

(3) To ensure that baggage for carriage on passenger flights, whether accompanied or unaccompanied, when originating from places other than the airport check-in counters is subjected to security control.

(4) To arrange for secure storage areas to be provided at airports serving international civil aviation, where mishandled baggage may be held until forwarded, claimed or disposed of according to the local laws.

(5) To take the necessary measures so that unidentified baggage is placed in a protected and isolated area until such time as it is ascertained that it does not contain any explosives or other dangerous device(s).

Personnel

Similarly, movement of unauthorised persons must be carefully supervised at airports at all times. The ICAO recommendations in Annex 17 for the contracting states are:

(1) to establish procedures and identity systems to prevent unauthorised access by persons or vehicles (a) airside or (b) any other areas which are important for security;
(2) to establish measures to ensure adequate supervision of movement of persons to and from the aircraft and to prevent unauthorised access to aircraft.

*Interceptions

If, while flying away happily over the UK or a foreign territory, you are required to alter your heading because, for example, you are approaching a danger area, or, in a more likely case, the nation on the surface below wants you to land, attempts will first be made to pass the instructions over radio. Failing contact on radio, an aircraft may be despatched to give you visual signals. The signals which most countries recognise, are these:

(1) Aircraft wishing you to follow him takes up a position slightly above and in front of you to your left, and rocks its wings. You acknowledge by rocking your wings. At night, the other aircraft additionally irregularly flashes its navigation lights. Your acknowledgement is the same.
(2) The intended message is that you are to follow him and land when he signals you to do so. After you have acknowledged him, he will make a slow level turn, normally to the left, on to the desired heading.
   (a) At the aerodrome of intended landing the other aircraft commences circling with its undercarriage down. Additionally, at night, it will show a steady landing light. You acknowledge it by following the same procedure, and proceed to land.
   (b) You may find that the aerodrome where the other aircraft wants you to land is not adequate. In this case you convey the message:
   by day: pass over the runway at height above 300 m (1000 ft) but not above 600 m (2000 ft) and rock the wings;
   by night: pass over the runway at height exceeding 300 m (1000 ft) but not exceeding 600 m (2000 ft) flashing landing lights as you pass over. If you are unable to land at the aerodrome because it is inadequate, it is for the other aircraft to decide what to do about you. It may take up position in front of you to the left and start all over again.
(3) Alternatively the aircraft may be merely taking you out of, say, a danger or prohibited area. In this case at an appropriate stage it will carry out an abrupt 'breakaway' manoeuvre, consisting of a climbing turn of 90° or more without crossing your line of flight. This means that you may now proceed and you acknowledge it by rocking your wings, day or night.
(4) Interceptions of civil aircraft are potentially hazardous situations and

nations should only use them as a last resort. You should respond to the intercepting aircraft's signals and if possible tell the Air Traffic Service Unit with whom you are in contact. Try to establish RTF contact with the intercepting aircraft or its control unit by making a general call on the emergency frequency 121.50 MHz. Give your identity and the nature of your flight. If 121.50 MHz produces no contact, try again if possible on emergency frequency 243 MHz.

(5) ON SSR, if equipped, select Mode A Code 7700 with Mode C, unless otherwise instructed by the appropriate Air Traffic Service Unit.

(6) Nevertheless under Article 9 of the Convention on International Civil Aviation, each contracting state reserves the right for reasons of military necessity or public safety, to restrict or prohibit the aircraft of other states from flying over certain areas of its territory. The Regulations of a state may prescribe the need to investigate the identity of aircraft. Accordingly it may be necessary to lead an aircraft of another state, which has been intercepted, away from a particular area (such as a prohibited area) or an intercepted aircraft may be required to land for security reasons at a designated aerodrome.

(7) The best means of avoidance of the risk of interception is by strict adherence to the flight plan and early and rapid clarification of any doubts about your identity through the appropriate ATS unit. As regards the latter, if you have established communication with the intercepting aircraft but there is a language problem, then nine key words should be used as appropriate:

CALLSIGN   MAYDAY   DESCEND   WILCO   REPEAT
CANNOT   AM LOST   LAND (. . . aerodrome) HIJACK*

* Circumstances may make this word unusable

Similarly the intercepting aircraft may use as key words:

CALLSIGN/FOLLOW/DESCEND/YOU LAND/PROCEED

(8) Remember that if the instructions received by radio conflict with the intercepting aircraft's visual signals, comply with the visual signals while seeking immediate clarification of the radio messages. Behave similarly if the radio messages from the intercepting aircraft differ from the communications from the ATS unit.

Notification of accidents

In conformity to Annex 13 to the Convention certain accidents become 'reportable' under UK legislation either under Civil Aviation (Investigation of Accidents) Regulations, or Air Navigation (Investigation of Air accidents involving Civil and Military Aircraft or Installations) Regulations. Under these two legislations, accidents under the following circumstances become 'reportable'.

An accident which occurs between the time when any person boards an aircraft with the intention of flight and such time as all persons have disembarked, and in consequence of the accident:

(a) any person suffers death or serious injury while in or upon the aircraft or by direct contact with any part of the aircraft or any part which has become detached from the aircraft or by direct exposure to jet blast; or

(b) the aircraft incurs damage or structural failure, other than:

   (i) engine failure or damage, when damage is limited to the engine, its cowling or accessories;

   (ii) damage limited to propellers, wing-tips, antennae, tyres, brakes, fairings, small dents or punctured holes in the aircraft skin;

   which would adversely affect its structural strength, performance or flight characteristics and would normally require major repair or replacement;

(c) the aircraft is missing or completely inaccessible.

What is meant by serious injury is spelt out in detail in the accident regulations. Death or serious injury from natural causes, or if self-inflicted or if suffered by a stowaway hiding 'outside areas normally available in flight to passengers and crew' are not reportable.

The notification is given by the commander of the aircraft, or if he is killed or incapacitated, the operator or any other person on whose behalf he was in command of the aircraft. The notification is made to the Chief Inspector, Accident Investigation Branch, Department of Transport, and, if the accident takes place in or over the UK, to the local police authorities in addition. The quickest means of communication are to be used to send the notification.

An 'incident' is any fortuitous or unexpected event, not being a 'reportable accident' by which the safety of an aircraft or any person is threatened.

The lessons to be learnt from accidents, incidents or occurrences are promulgated by the CAA. A General Aviation Safety Information Leaflet (GASIL) with a distinctive purple top margin is widely distributed free monthly (including to every UK flying school and club). Reports of occurrences are presented 'in a dis-identified summary containing the relevant factual information'. In most cases, the CAA experts then offer comment and advice on appropriate remedial measures.

Test 1

(1) Minimum weather conditions for a VFR flight below FL 100 in controlled Airspace Classes D and E are given in terms of minimum cloud separation vertically, horizontally and a certain minimum flight visibility. These distances are respectively:

    (a) 2000 ft   1500 m   5 km
    (b) 500 ft   1800 m   8 km
    (c) 1000 ft   1500 m   5 km

(2) One of the following is required in order to obtain clearance for IFR flight in controlled airspace:

    (a) a commercial licence;
    (b) an instrument rating;
    (c) a night rating.

(3) Within all Controlled Airspace, air traffic clearance is required for:

    (a) all types of flights;
    (b) IFR at night;
    (c) VFR in daylight.

(4) Which is the appropriate flight level in IFR if the magnetic track is 269°?

    (a) 55
    (b) 60
    (c) 65

(5) Flying at FL 70, in IMC your magnetic track is between:

    (a) 000° to 089° inclusive;
    (b) 180° to 270° inclusive;
    (c) 180° to 269° inclusive.

(6) Flying at 2000 ft, outside controlled airspace, visibility 4 nm. The aircraft's magnetic track is decided by:

    (a) the passenger;

(b) air traffic control unit;

(c) the pilot.

(7) An aircraft is flying IFR outside controlled airspace, altitude 4000 ft. It must:

(a) fly quadrantals;

(b) fly under air traffic control instructions;

(c) fly under FIR controller's instructions.

(8) When flying on an advisory route and utilising advisory service it is necessary to file a flight plan:

(a) only if flying under IFR;

(b) only if flying within controlled airspace;

(c) always.

(9) The ground signal meaning 'manoeuvring area is poor and pilots should exercise special care' is:

(a) red square panel with a yellow strip along one diagonal;

(b) red square panel with yellow strips along both diagonals;

(c) white dumb-bell with black strip.

(10) A danger area which is always active during prescribed hours throughout the weekdays is shown on the authorised danger area chart by:

(a) solid red outline;

(b) solid blue outline;

(c) solid blue outline marked Schedule (2).

(11) During an initial climb in uncontrolled airspace, the pilot:

(a) may use any desired setting;

(b) must use 1013.2 setting;

(c) must use local QNH only.

(12) An airway is:

(a) 5 nm wide;

(b) 10 nm wide;

(c) 15 nm wide.

(13) A controlled airspace is:

(a) an airspace within FIR within which ATC service is provided;

(b) an airspace within UIR within which ATC service is provided;

(c) an airspace within FIR/UIR within which ATC service is provided.

(14) To obtain terrain clearance while en route:

    (a) QNE setting is used;
    (b) QFF setting is used;
    (c) Regional QNH is used.

(15) You must fly quadrantals when flying above 3000 ft:

    (a) only when IFR and inside controlled airspace;
    (b) only when IFR and inside or outside controlled airspace;
    (c) only when IFR and outside controlled airspace.

(16) When flying in an advisory airspace:

    (a) ground control is exercised over the aircraft;
    (b) separation is provided from other known traffic;
    (c) you may be given headings to steer.

(17) The controlling authority for a TMA generally is:

    (a) the controlling authority of the main airfield in the TMA;
    (b) ATCC;
    (c) zone controller.

(18) At a UK aerodrome the altimeter check can be carried out:

    (a) on an apron;
    (b) in flight clearance office;
    (c) in flight briefing room.

(19) An aircraft is approaching an aerodrome which is below TMA. It is at transition altitude. The appropriate altimeter setting is:

    (a) regional QNH;
    (b) regional QFE;
    (c) Aerodrome QNH.

(20) A flight plan must be filed:

    (a) by a private pilot when flying beyond a certain distance over the water from the coast;
    (b) 30 minutes before taxi clearance is required;
    (c) on all occasions when a girl friend is carried on board.

(21) An airmiss report must be followed up by form CA 1094:

    (a) within 7 days of the incident;

(b) within 7 days of the date that the pilot recovered from the shock;

(c) immediately on landing.

(22) Red and green stars fired from ground towards an aircraft signifies:

(a) the aircraft has violated a danger area and that it should land at a suitable aerodrome;

(b) the aircraft is approaching a danger area and should alter heading;

(c) 5th of November is around.

(23) In the UK air navigation obstructions are lighted if they are:

(a) 300 ft or higher, agl;

(b) 150 ft or higher, agl;

(c) 300 ft or higher, and when the CAA has been notified of their existence.

(24) A continuous red beam directed to an aircraft means:

(a) owing to the aerodrome being unserviceable, landing should be made elsewhere;

(b) aircraft is prohibited from landing for time being and previous permission is cancelled;

(c) give way to the other aircraft and continue circling.

(25) If a pilot lands at an aerodrome other than that given in the flight plan:

(a) he must inform the original destination within 30 minutes of his ETA there;

(b) he must inform the original destination within 30 minutes of his landing elsewhere;

(c) once an aerodrome has been designated in the flight plan he cannot land elsewhere.

(26) In the UK the Upper Flight Information Region is established. It extends:

(a) from ground level, having no upper limit;

(b) above flight level 250;

(c) above flight level 245.

(27) One of the requirements to fly IFR in controlled airspace is that:

(a) it carries a pilot;

(b) it is flown 1000 ft above all obstacles within 5 nm of the track;

(c) it is flown 1500 ft above all obstacles within 15 nm of the track.

(28) When flying over the sea you must not fly closer than a certain distance to a vessel. The distance is:

(a) 2000 ft
(b) 1000 ft
(c) 500 ft.

(29) Smoking is prohibited in an aircraft:

(a) when 'no smoking' sign is displayed;
(b) during take-offs and landings;
(c) during take-offs and landings and when flying through turbulent air.

(30) When carrying out a circuit at an aerodrome, all turns are normally:

(a) right-handed;
(b) left-handed;
(c) there is no set rule and instructions must be obtained from the ATC.

(31) When flying at night you observe another aircraft moving at right angles and crossing your track from left to right. You would be seeing its:

(a) red light;
(b) green light;
(c) white light.

(32) When two aircraft are approaching head on:

(a) both alter heading to right;
(b) bigger aircraft alters its heading to right;
(c) smaller aircraft alters its heading to right.

(33) With certain exceptions, on every occasion when you fly you must carry:

(a) technical log book;
(b) Certificate of Registration;
(c) Certificate of Airworthiness.

(34) In the UK while navigating by visual reference to a landmark, e.g. a railway line, the rule is to keep to such landmark:

(a) to the left of the aircraft;
(b) to the right of the aircraft;
(c) below the aircraft.

(35) The authoritative map for danger areas in the UK is:

(a) ICAO approved topographical map;
(b) map of danger areas published by the CAA;
(c) any navigational map approved by the CAA.

(36) If while in flight at night you observe a white flashing light ahead of you, which is getting closer, you are:

    (a) observing a captive balloon;
    (b) approaching an obstruction, such as a tall building;
    (c) overtaking an aircraft.

(37) A Customs aerodrome is:

    (a) open day and night;
    (b) open day only;
    (c) open during published hours.

(38) A passenger who is drunk:

    (a) shall be refused permission to board the aircraft;
    (b) shall be permitted on board only if accompanied by a companion who would undertake responsibility for him;
    (c) shall be interrogated by the commander as to the whereabouts of the cheap liquor stores.

(39) An aircraft may not fly over an assembly of over 1000 persons within a distance of:

    (a) 3000 ft;
    (b) 1000 ft;
    (c) 1000 m.

(40) The responsibility for ensuring that the radio equipment is serviceable prior to take-off is that of the:

    (a) co-pilot;
    (b) commander;
    (c) radio officer.

(41) The letter 'C' displayed in black against a yellow background indicates:

    (a) place where cafeteria and refreshments are available;
    (b) place where air traffic control unit is located;
    (c) place where the pilot of visiting aircraft may report.

(42) When flying over an aerodrome where no ATC is operational for the time being, the pilot should:

    (a) keep clear of the cloud and not descend below 500 ft above the aerodrome elevation;
    (b) keep 500 ft below the cloud;

(c) keep 500 ft above the cloud.

(43) When one taxiing flying machine wishes to overtake another machine, the overtaking machine shall alter course to:

(a) the right;
(b) the left;
(c) right or left.

(44) An authorised person may require production of the Certificate of Airworthiness. The responsibility for production of this lies with:

(a) the operator, who should produce it within 6 months;
(b) the commander, who should produce it within 5 days;
(c) the commander, who should produce it within reasonable time.

(45) The Personal Licence, when not required to be carried in the aircraft and demanded by the authorised person, should be produced by the licence holder:

(a) within reasonable time;
(b) within 5 days;
(c) within 7 days.

(46) The marshalling signal 'arms down, palms facing inwards, arms swung from extended position inwards' means:

(a) this bay;
(b) turn to port;
(c) insert chocks.

(47) An aeroplane has landed at an aerodrome without runways. The pilot of the following aircraft, with reference to the first aircraft, shall:

(a) leave it clear on his left and subsequently turn left;
(b) leave it clear on his left and subsequently turn right;
(c) leave it clear on his right and subsequently turn left.

(48) The last aerodrome that, generally, you take off from for flight abroad is:

(a) health aerodrome;
(b) Customs aerodrome;
(c) public aerodrome.

(49) The aeronautical ground light beacons at civil aerodromes show:

(a) a two-letter identification code in green;

(b) a two-letter identification code in red;

(c) a rotating red and green.

(50) For flight exceeding 500 nm the following minimum notice is required by the met office:

(a) 4 hours;

(b) 2 hours;

(c) 1 hour.

Answers to test No. 1

(1)(c)	(18)(a)	(35)(b)
(2)(b)	(19)(c)	(36)(c)
(3)(b)	(20)(b)	(37)(c)
(4)(b)	(21)(a)	(38)(a)
(5)(a)	(22)(b)	(39)(a)
(6)(c)	(23)(a)	(40)(b)
(7)(a)	(24)(c)	(41)(c)
(8)(c)	(25)(a)	(42)(a)
(9)(a)	(26)(c)	(43)(b)
(10)(a)	(27)(b)	(44)(c)
(11)(a)	(28)(c)	(45)(b)
(12)(b)	(29)(a)	(46)(c)
(13)(c)	(30)(b)	(47)(a)
(14)(c)	(31)(b)	(48)(b)
(15)(c)	(32)(a)	(49)(a)
(16)(b)	(33)(c)	(50)(a)
(17)(b)	(34)(a)	

Test 2

(1) The height of the airfield is determined by:

    (a) the highest point on the landing area;
    (b) the lowest point on the manoeuvring area;
    (c) the highest point of the runway mostly in use.

(2) The minimum number of crew that must be carried is laid down in:

    (a) the Rules of the Air;
    (b) the Air Navigation Order;
    (c) the Certificate of Airworthiness.

(3) Runway Visual Range is reported when the visibility falls below:

    (a) 1100 ft;
    (b) 1100 yd;
    (c) 1100 m.

(4) Entries in a log book are made in:

    (a) ink or indelible pencil;
    (b) red ink only;
    (c) black ink only.

(5) On runways having an adverse uphill slope the take-off distance increases at the rate of:

    (a) 10% for 1° slope;
    (b) 10% for 2° slope;
    (c) 1% for 10° slope.

(6) Aircraft flying to or from places abroad may cross the UK coastline:

    (a) only at a reporting point;
    (b) only at the point designated in the flight plan;
    (c) at any point which is not a danger area and the crossing does not infringe any other rule.

(7) At aerodrome where Aerodrome Flight information Service only operates:

    (a) pilot will have to make up his own mind which runway to use;

    (b) pilot will be guided by the landing T in the signals area;

    (c) pilot must obey landing T instructions.

(8) EAT is the time that:

    (a) an arriving aircraft will be cleared to leave his position in the stack;

    (b) an aircraft will leave en route holding point;

    (c) an arriving aircraft will be cleared to leave the lowest level of the holding stack and commence approach to land.

(9) At a certain altitude and above, when cabin pressure falls below a certain level, oxygen must be used. This pressure level is:

    (a) less than 700 mb;

    (b) 700 mb or less;

    (c) that which would prevail at 10 000 ft.

(10) The maximum flying time permitted under the law is:

    (a) 100 hr during a period of 28 consecutive days;

    (b) 100 hr during a period of one month;

    (c) 1500 hour during one single year.

(11) 'Approach to landing' is being made when the flight descends below:

    (a) 1000 ft above critical height;

    (b) 1000 ft above all obstacles;

    (c) 1000 ft above highest point on the manoeuvring area.

(12) The weather information passed by approach control to arriving aircraft is given in the following order:

    (a) cloud ceiling – RVR;

    (b) cloud – weather – surface W/V – visibility;

    (c) surface W/V – visibility – weather – cloud.

(13) 'Visual contact approach' is an approach:

    (a) which is completed IFR in VMC;

    (b) by an IFR flight when part or all of the procedure is completed with visual reference to the terrain;

    (c) which may be forced upon pilots who are strangers to the aerodrome.

(14) QFE value of 1010.6 mb will be passed to the pilot as:

(a) 1010.6;
(b) 1010;
(c) 1010.5.

(15) 'Break-in Areas' shall be marked on all public transport aircraft whose maximum total weight authorised:

(a) exceeds 3600 kg;
(b) is 3600 kg or more;
(c) is 5700 kg or more.

(16) The Runway Visual Range Markers are coloured:

(a) red and black;
(b) red and white;
(c) black and white.

(17) A departure message consists of:

(a) DEP – a/c ident – ETD;
(b) DEP – time of departure – company's name;
(c) DEP – a/c ident – actual time of departure.

(18) When in an aerodrome circuit, base leg call is made:

(a) on completion of the turn on to the base leg;
(b) at the end of the downwind leg;
(c) when established on the base leg.

(19) An aircraft may be allowed to land on a runway before the preceding aircraft has cleared it, provided that:

(a) it is during daylight hours only;
(b) it is during daylight and night hours only;
(c) it is night hours only.

(20) If, when waiting at a runway holding point prior to take-off, a navigation light is found to have failed, the pilot:

(a) may take off if he receives take-off clearance from ATC;
(b) may take off provided that the anti-collision light is still working;
(c) must not depart until the failed light is repaired or replaced.

(21) A licence holder who suffers an injury making him incapable of undertaking his duties under the licence should inform the CAA. This should be done:

(a) when 20 days have elapsed;
(b) immediately;
(c) within 20 days.

(22) The load sheet is signed by:

(a) the supervisor only;
(b) the commander only;
(c) both the supervisor and the commander.

(23) Two aircraft are departing from the same aerodrome and the lateral separation is provided immediately after take-off. The separation minimum at take-off is:

(a) 1 minute;
(b) 2 minutes;
(c) 5 minutes.

(24) En route terrain clearance provided by radar is:

(a) 1000 ft above the highest obstacle within 10 nm either side of the airway centreline;
(b) 1500 ft above the highest obstacle within 10 nm either side of the airway centreline;
(c) 1500 ft above highest obstacle within 30 nm of the track when the aircraft is not flying on airways.

(25) If navigation equipment fails the correct procedure is:

(a) to leave the controlled airspace immediately;
(b) inform ATC who may authorise the flight to continue in the controlled airspace;
(c) to ensure it is made serviceable at the next landing.

(26) An arrival message is not required in the case of a flight:

(a) from Rome to London, the aircraft in fact landing at Manchester;
(b) from Rome to London, the aircraft landing at London;
(c) from New York to London, aircraft landing at Manchester.

(27) Above 29 000 ft the flight separation is:

(a) 500 ft;
(b) 1000 ft;
(c) 2000 ft.

(28) A SIGMET message contains:

    (a) warning of severe weather;
    (b) routine weather report;
    (c) important message for VIPs on board.

(29) Rules regarding the Upper Heyford Mandatory Radio Area:

    (a) are observed only when promulgated in NOTAM;
    (b) are enforced permanently;
    (c) are not applicable outside the notified hours of watch.

(30) In the UK, definition of 'night' includes the period:

    (a) half an hour after sunset to half an hour before sunrise at surface level;
    (b) half an hour after sunset to half an hour before sunrise at the aircraft's flight level;
    (c) half an hour after sunset to half an hour after sunrise.

(31) For load sheet purposes, an average weight of the passengers and crew members may be used:

    (a) at the commander's discretion;
    (b) when majority of the passengers are not excessively fat;
    (c) when the total seating capacity is twelve or more.

(32) The ground-air signal put up by the survivors requiring medical assistance is:

    (a) N;
    (b) X;
    (c) Y.

(33) The recommended times for the operation of Dinghy Radio are:

    (a) for three minutes on the hour, and hour plus 30;
    (b) for three minutes, hour plus 15, and hour plus 45;
    (c) on the hour.

(34) The responsibility for maintaining the Operations Manual up to date rests with:

    (a) operator;
    (b) the commander;
    (c) the CAA.

(35) When average weights are taken for passengers and crew members for the load sheet purposes, the weight of an adult female is:

(a) 39 kg;
(b) 75 kg;
(c) 65 kg.

(36) On an approach to an aerodrome with PAPI, if you see 2 whites and 2 reds, you are:

(a) slightly high;
(b) slightly low;
(c) on correct path.

(37) The correct procedure for an aircraft in distress is to:

(a) first call on the frequency in use and then on 121.5 MHz;
(b) call on 121.5 straight away;
(c) wait until someone calls the aircraft first.

(38) For a public transport aircraft, the weather minima laid down are:

(a) cloud ceiling and RVR for landing;
(b) critical height and RVR for landing;
(c) critical height and RVR for take-off.

(39) The weather observations sent out by an aircraft are in code:

(a) METAR;
(b) AIREP;
(c) TAF.

(40) The following accident is 'reportable':

(a) a passenger climbing up the stairs attached to the aircraft, slips and breaks his leg;
(b) aircraft on landing bursts a tyre;
(c) passenger on way out to the aircraft, slips on the apron and breaks his leg.

(41) VOR, ADF and DME must be carried when the flight is in:

(a) both controlled area and control zones;
(b) control zones only;
(c) IFR in controlled airspace.

(42) An aircraft crossing another's track at the same level, the time separation will be:

    (a) 10 minutes;
    (b) 5 minutes;
    (c) 2 minutes.

(43) On an instrument runway the fixed distance markings are placed:

    (a) 600 m apart;
    (b) every 150 m;
    (c) 300 m from the threshold.

(44) A Class B bearing given by a ground DF station is accurate within:

    (a) $\pm 2°$;
    (b) $\pm 5°$;
    (c) $\pm 10°$.

(45) A flight plan must be filed when undertaking a flight:

    (a) beyond 10 nm over the sea;
    (b) beyond 10 nm over the sea and over mountainous area;
    (c) in notified controlled airspace.

(46) The flight information service provided within an FIR may include:

    (a) serviceability of aerodromes and their navigational aids;
    (b) serviceability of aerodromes and the headings to steer to get there;
    (c) serviceability of aerodromes and the heights to fly to get there.

(47) A white light flashed from ATC to a taxiing aircraft means:

    (a) give way to the other aircraft on the taxiway;
    (b) return to your starting point on the aerodrome;
    (c) you have right of way over other aircraft on the taxiway.

(48) One of the conditions that must be complied with when carrying out a simulated instrument flight is that:

    (a) the aircraft has dual controls;
    (b) one extra person is carried in the second seat;
    (c) one extra person is carried in the second seat and if field of vision is not adequate, a third person is carried.

(49) The red and green wing tip navigation lights must be at least of:

   (a) 20 candela;
   (b) 3 candela;
   (c) 5 candela.

(50) An aircraft lands at aerodrome A and requires replacement of a part included in the Certificate of Airworthiness. Since it cannot obtain the certificate of release to service at A, it flies to B. The commander of the aircraft should notify the CAA of the flight from A to B within:

   (a) a reasonable time;
   (b) as soon as the aircraft returns to the UK;
   (c) ten days.

Answers to test 2

(1)(a)	(11)(a)	(21)(b)	(31)(c)	(41)(c)
(2)(c)	(12)(c)	(22)(c)	(32)(b)	(42)(a)
(3)(c)	(13)(b)	(23)(a)	(33)(b)	(43)(c)
(4)(a)	(14)(b)	(24)(c)	(34)(a)	(44)(b)
(5)(b)	(15)(a)	(25)(b)	(35)(c)	(45)(c)
(6)(c)	(16)(c)	(26)(b)	(36)(c)	(46)(a)
(7)(a)	(17)(c)	(27)(c)	(37)(a)	(47)(b)
(8)(c)	(18)(a)	(28)(a)	(38)(b)	(48)(a)
(9)(b)	(19)(a)	(29)(c)	(39)(b)	(49)(c)
(10)(a)	(20)(c)	(30)(a)	(40)(a)	(50)(c)

Test 3

Rules of the air and lights

(1) You are flying at night and observe the following light/lights of another aircraft, flying at the same level at range approximately 5 nm. Does a risk of collision exist, and if so, what action would you take?

Relative bearing	Light/lights seen
(a) 040°	Red
(b) 320°	Red and Green
(c) 340°	Green
(d) 040°	Green
(e) 000°	Red and Green
(f) 000°	Green

(2) State what action, if any, you would take in the following circumstances. Assume that the range of the other aircraft is 5 nm and that both aircraft are approximately at the same level.

Light/lights seen	Relative bearing	Subsequent observation
(a) White flashing in alternation with red and green	050°	Relative bearing increases
(b) White flashing in alternation with white	005°	Relative bearing remains constant
(c) White flashing in alternation with red and green	360°	Relative bearing remains constant
(d) White flashing alternately with green	310°	Relative bearing decreases

(3) You are flying on a heading (T) of 290° when you see a green light at a relative bearing of 320°. Between what headings could the other aircraft possibly be flying?

(4) You are flying on a heading of 180(T) when you sight a white light on a relative bearing of 350°. Between what two headings could the other aircraft possibly be flying?

(5) Flying at night you see red and green lights of another aircraft, at a range of approximately 4 nm and at about your altitude, on a relative bearing of 085°.
    (a) Is there a risk of collision?
    (b) If so, what action would you take?

Answers to Test 3

(1) (a) Yes, the risk of collision must be presumed. The aircraft might be converging on you from your starboard. The other aircraft has the right of way. Therefore, at appropriate time, you should alter heading to the right and pass him.

    (b) There is no risk of collision since you are passing the centreline of the other aircraft. In another instant you will stop seeing red and green and start seeing red only.

    (c) Yes, there is a risk of collision. The other aircraft might be converging on you from your port side. You have the right of way and the action is to maintain heading and speed and keep a look out.

    (d) There is no risk of collision; the other aircraft is going away from you.

    (e) Risk of collision exists; the two aircraft are approaching head on. At appropriate time, both alter heading to right.

    (f) There is no risk of collision. The other aircraft is either crossing your track, or, at the other extreme, approaching you from the opposite direction. In this case, however, it cannot be approaching head on.

(2) (a) There is no risk of collision. Since you are seeing both its red and green lights, you are crossing the other aircraft's flight path. The next instant you will be out of its way, as is confirmed in subsequent observations.

    (b) In this case you must presume risk of collision. The chances are that you are overtaking the other aircraft. Action for you is to alter heading right to overtake. You must not alter heading to the left to resume original track until you have passed the other aircraft and are well clear of it.

    (c) Yes, there is a risk of collision. Aircraft approaching head on. Alter heading right.

    (d) A green light on your left raises a presumption of risk. However, since subsequent observations show that the relative bearing decreases, there can be no risk of collision. You are simply going ahead of the other aircraft.

(3) Hdg(T)   290
    R.B.   <u>320</u>
    T.B.   610
    –   <u>360</u>
                250
    –   <u>180</u>
                070 – One limit
    –   <u>110</u>
                320 – Other limit

Ans: 070° to 320° through North.

(4) Hdg(T)   180
     R.B.   350
     T.B.   530
     –   360
                    170

170 ± 70 (180 – 110) = 240 and 100.

Ans: 240° to 100° through South.

(5) (a) No risk of collision.
    (b) You are crossing the other aircraft's track so no action is required other than keeping a good look-out.

Index